DRINKING WHILE WRITING WHILE WRITING WHILE DRINKING

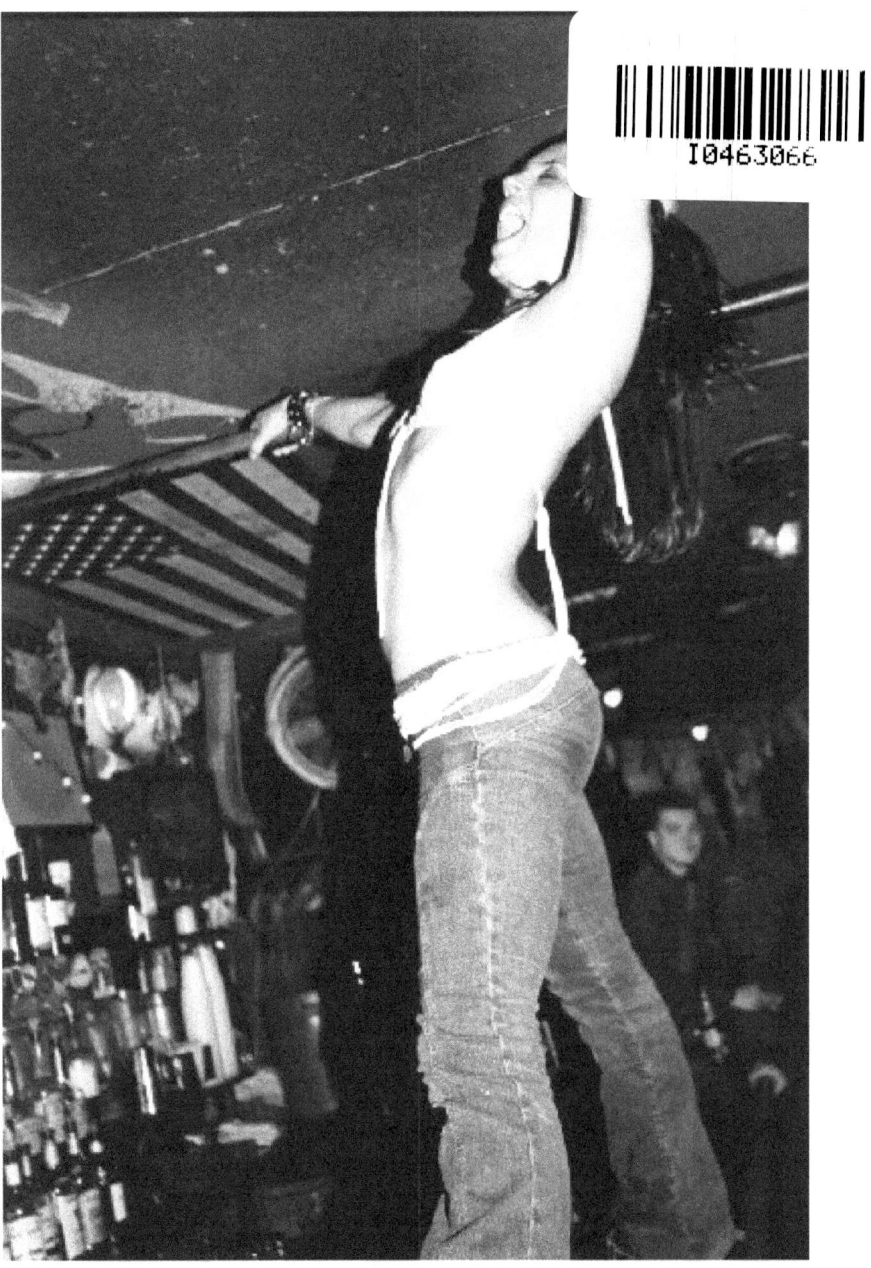

Words by Crazy Legs Conti   Photos by Erik Madden

A DRUNKARD'S GOODBYE TO HOGS AND HEIFERS AND FUCK YOU NEW YORK CITY

By Crazy Legs Conti

08/18/2015

A dive bar's value is not in its cheap rotgut beer or discount hootch, but its currency of folklore; The famous rummies who bellied to the bar and the ubiquitous drink-slingers who concurrently rule and serve, the photos of shellacked and ebrious times that stain the walls, the hypnotic hallucinated alcohol-soaked recollections of the late nights, early mornings, and daydream afternoons of drinking that sublimate into the grimy dust strewn stale air. The dive bar's folklore is its stories and when they tear it all down to Hell, its stories are its only memory.

I moved to New York City in 1993, a year after the biker dive bar Hogs and Heifers opened. Minus a year in Northern California teaching Middle School, I have lived in New York City for over twenty years. Twenty years of the daily grind won't get me singing Sinatra or praising the majestic skyline - clinging to the cliched magic of being a true "New Yawker." My feelings on the city are more complex, akin to Lou Reed's thoughts in the documentary, "Blue in the Face" when he says he is sick of New York, that he is done, and that he is leaving. Asked, how long has he felt that way, deadpan to camera he answers, "Thirty five years." Lou didn't get out, but I might someday. I wasn't in Paris in the twenties but I get that it was always better ten years ago. That I should have been here before it all changed, before it all became the same. A homogenized culture of banks and unreal estate that pushes the artists and interesting folks further and further out until they end up in Detroit. I get the easy rap but the ATMs at the bank where the 2nd Ave Deli used to be don't dispense matzo ball soup from the money slots and there is nothing punk about $600 sweaters instead of $6 sweating to the music where CBGBs existed. Why cry over the spoiled rancid milk that NYC's trendy latte froth? The first time I walked into Hogs and Heifers there was a thumbtacked Polaroid of Charles Bukowski look alike drinking at the very bar - glass aloft, his face a rictus of deranged happiness as if to say, "I don't wish you were here but I'm glad I am."

Sure, the meatpacking district was more authentic, dangerous, and fun when leather clad daddies drank at a dark bars, bloodstained butcher coat third-shift workers hung animal carcasses, and transvestite hookers added the flash to the neighborhood, their mismatched high heels clacking the cobblestones after furtive blow jobs on decrepit stairways. I suppose now the reality TV show wannabes, also in their giraffe high heels, give costly blow jobs at the night clubs, lounges, and hotel bars but I have no interest in those vapid chicks, velvet ropes, dress codes, or dying bottle service. In the last decade the only two places worth visiting this side of the High Line are The Corner Bistro and Hogs and Heifers. Hogs and Heifers closes on August 23rd and I f'ing swear to you in this writing, if the Corner Bistro bunks I will disappear from New York City forever.

I use to do the triple back in the day - three bars an evening. You needed about a hundred bucks to do it right, twice that if you were trying to get laid. My favorite bar of all time, The Village Idiot, had a bar that slanted in two directions downwards, like most of its patrons, and sitting in the wrong spot would lead to beer stained shorts as the swill dripped too slow to notice - like a glacier paced cum stain. In the 90s one could buy three goldfish for a dollar and feed them to the snapping turtles in the only illuminated part of the bar in the front. That was actually not the most politically incorrect item on the menu - when needing bartenders the chalkboard outside would read, "Sluts wanted. Apply within." Despite that ominous job description, the bartenders preceded the tattooed tough sexy girl movement and were intelligent beauties who could pour and drink whiskey while black electrical tape covered their nipples. Often the girls would make $300 in one sixty minute run during power hour, as the construction workers drank their liquid lunch before heading back to operate heavy machinery. I spent five thanksgivings in that bar and on the holiday, went home with the bartender twice - Thanks, giving, indeed. My only religion is dive bars and Mary Dawn, bartending topless, her cowboy hat low-riding like her clingy stretch jeans, was the patron saint of construction workers and short order cooks. I spent the 2003 citywide blackout there and when the lights came on only on the north side of 14th street, we exited to cross the street to a still darkened bar, to party like it was last night. The typical greedy rent hike for trendy improvement made the closing night bittersweet and I asked Tom the owner if I could wear the dirt covered sombrero tacked to the wall. He drunkenly slobbered, but appropriately said, "Let's just leave everything where it is." Still, he ended up selling the "Creature of the Black Lagoon" pinball machine to my buddy, Levi - the #2 pinball guy in New York State. The machine had not seen daylight in twenty years so the artwork was more pristine than any other game of it's kind but the change box kept producing fruit flies years after it was removed from the bar and it's perfume lingered - the stench of the Village Idiot - stale brew, burnt hair, and puke. The machine looked amazing but its core was rotten; a microcosm of the city perhaps.

Red Rock West was the rock-and-roll version of the country western music dives and is now replaced by the crappiest pizza place in NYC. The bouncers, except for my buddy Johnny Wacko (with "Fuck" tattooed on his upper lip, and "You" on the bottom) were all giants - whether it was steroids or Paul Bunyan in a future life, you didn't fuck around around the behemoths. The bartenders were more ecdysiasts than at The Village Idiot, more concerned with the pageantry of fire blowing than taking shots themselves, but the exceptions were always mesmerizing - like Kimmie, who worked the dive bar circuit, grabbing a bottle of beer she just served to some guy, and standing on the bar, licking the frothing foam lustfully before pouring it's contents down the front of her tight jeans. I guess it got her wet. It worked for me. Red Rock West did big business during Fleet Week and my long-haired buddy Dinshaw and I would dress as sailors figuring correctly that the drunk chicks loved guys in uniform, but couldn't remember which guy was which because they all looked the same. The dreadlocked hippy and scraggly rock star were easier to find on the dance floor where over-the-pants hand jobs were simpler than the Lambada. I met a great older swingers couple there whose rekindling their romance by letting random barflies bang the wife while the husband watched. They were the most life content people I knew. The community of the bar, despite being miscreants, was inspiring - sort of a gathering low class self-help gurus. Red Rock tried to go the reality TV route - last bartender standing audition competition shows - but networks didn't want it and public access television had morphed from Robin Byrd's breasts to 1-900 phone lines to ads in the pages of "Screw Magazine." With the internet in it's infancy, person-to-person New York filth was on the decline and Red Rock West was there for me every weekend and many weeknights and then it was gone.

Hogs and Heifers is the best known and authentic stalwart of the dive bar Meatpacking District trilogy. It's folklore has always been confusing - not the bullshit PR spin of Julia Roberts bra hanging above the bar or Hasslehoff falling down drunk a lot. Sure, that happened much as pre-cellphones on any night, I would see a dozen absolutely breathtaking beauties, civilian drinkers mind you, get atop the bar and show their tits, throw a bra to the pile, do a shot and dance. Cellphone cameras ended that, leaving only the country music blaring and the choreographed bartenders' shitkickers slamming the mottled wood of the bar. The folklore that my spongy brain can't quite recall as fact or fiction, but relegated to slurring oral history, is whether Melissa Gilbert, who wrote "Eat, Pray, Love" worked at Hogs or just at Coyote Ugly on the East Side. She wrote the "Vanity Fair" article that Hollywood's Jerry Bruckheimer optioned for a movie set in the world of female bartenders with bigger dreams than the smaller dive bars where they worked. The notion of "coyote ugly" - chewing one's arm off instead of waking last night's drunk decision lying next to you in bed, was deemed the better title despite that the resulting film was really more about Hogs and Heifers. A better title for Melissa Gilbert's early work might have been, "Drink, Puke, Lust." I like Coyote Ugly and still drink there, weathering the smell all these years, from the smoking ban (now your clothes don't smell smoky, but instead acrid, like Yagermeister) to it's current aroma of the overwhelming B.O. of bike messengers battling the perfume of foreign tourists. What's in a name? Coyote Ugly would franchise, largely due to the movie's notoriety, but also the fierce vision of a feisty female owner, and like DVDs to VHS, create fuzzy versions in cities around America and the world. I've been to a few - New Orleans is fine but there are better bars in NOLA to drink in. The Florida ones are faux dive bars and I was thrown out of Vegas due to a dress code that disallowed shorts despite me wearing a vest and ascot. I'll pass on the Coyote Ugly copies and still believe Hogs and Heifers to be the original. Now also owned by a powerful woman, the Hogs and Heifers Las Vegas outlet is a perfect wonder in the Fremont Experience district of old Vegas and is where most of the memorabilia will end up as the rent increase at New York City's flagship sends the space hurtling towards an unnecessary fashion boutique, fast food location, or bank. It all goes - Julia Roberts bra, the stalactites of dust around the ceiling fans, the plexiglas encased hunting photos, the hundreds of construction, civil service, law enforcement, and firefighting union patches, helmets, and paraphernalia. It's the antithesis of the historical artifacts at McSorely's - this crap is more representative of a singular inebriated moment - the handing of something with no monetary value but only maudlin sentimentality, from grungy owner to a dive bar beauty behind the bar. Everything on the walls and hanging off the taxidermic animals is a booze-stained love letter. The Bukowski-esque Polaroid was stolen long ago but the thumbtack is still up. It all goes away fading like the end of a Johnny Cash song on the flip card jukebox.

I don't think Ken Kesey made it to Hogs and Heifers but the Merry Prankster spirit is alive in my absinthe vapor thoughts. Kesey's quote, from I believe, his OZ-like play, Twister seems to fit these dive bar end of days...

"And one day the King's most loyal servant came into the royal chambers and said, "Your Majesty, all of the kingdom's wheat has been infested with a fungus that turns the people crazy when they eat it!" The King sadly contemplated this news then replied, "If we are going to be able to understand the people, then you and I must consume the fungus and become crazy too. But before we partake of the grain, let us make a mark on each other's forehead so that later, when we see one another, we will know that we chose to become insane, while everybody else is just crazy." - Ken Kesey

...and with that I am off to Hogs and Heifers for my last afternoon drinking there. Maybe the rosy glow sunset beyond the High Line will be visible as the heavy ramshackle door swings open and shut but I don't need to look out at sunset, to know what comes next. On August 24th, 2015 the door will be shuttered to scrapheap oblivion and only darkness will follow.

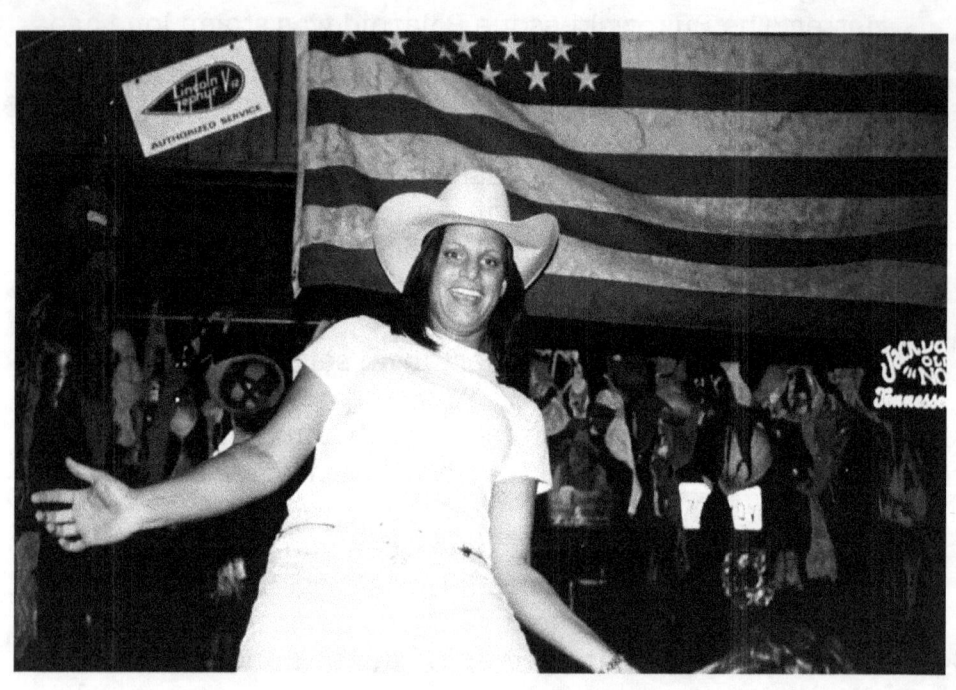

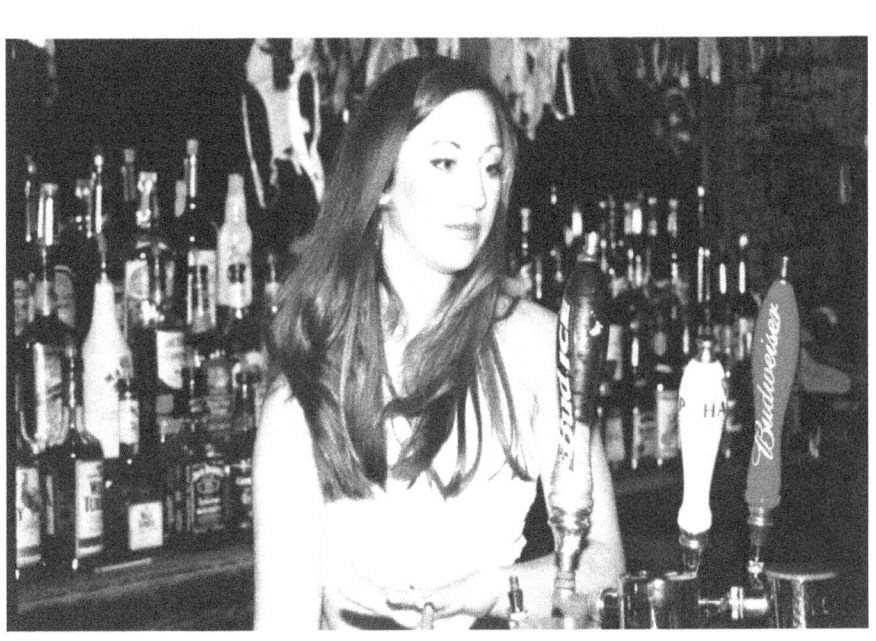

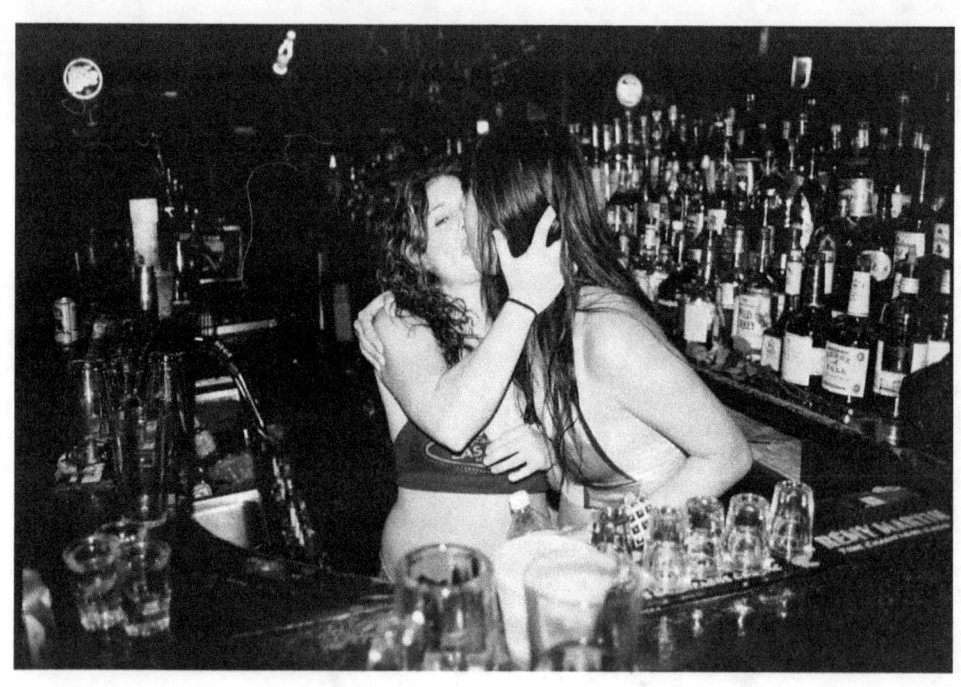

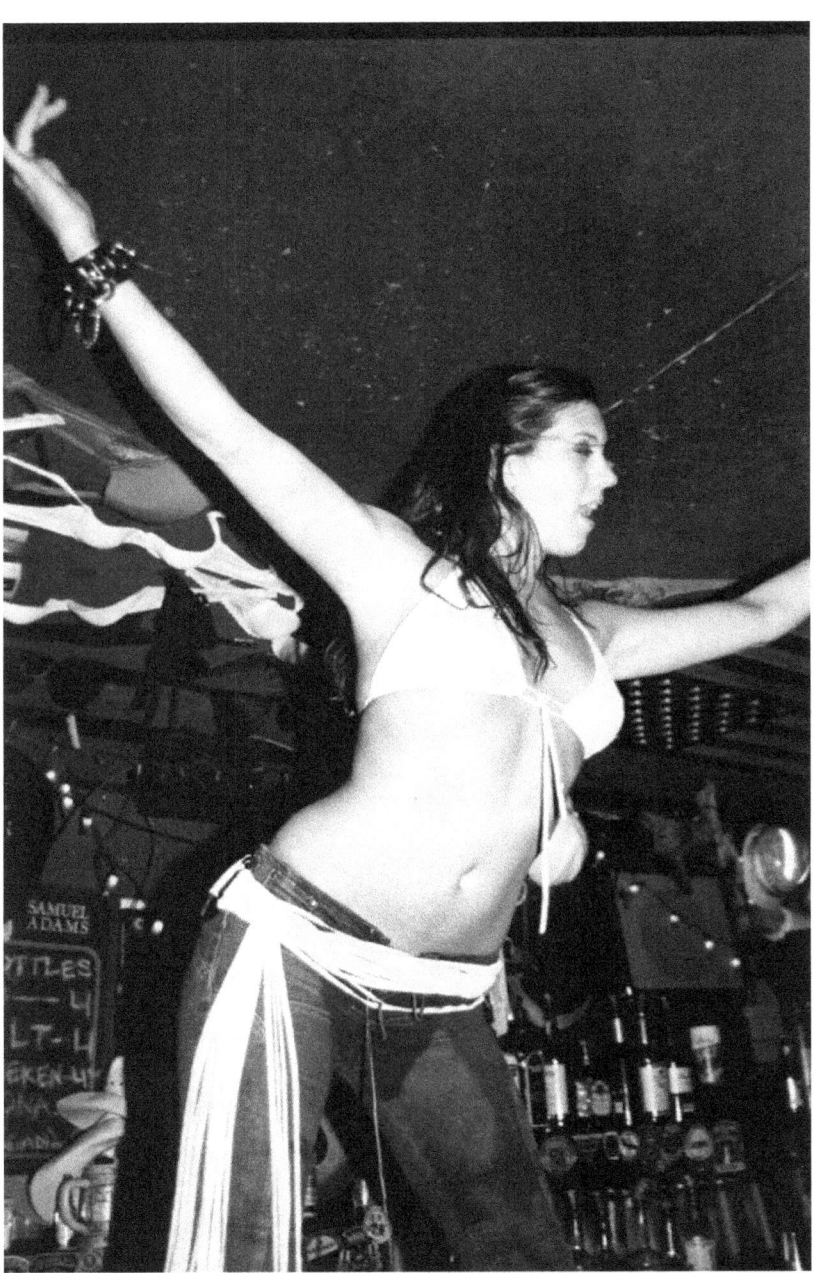

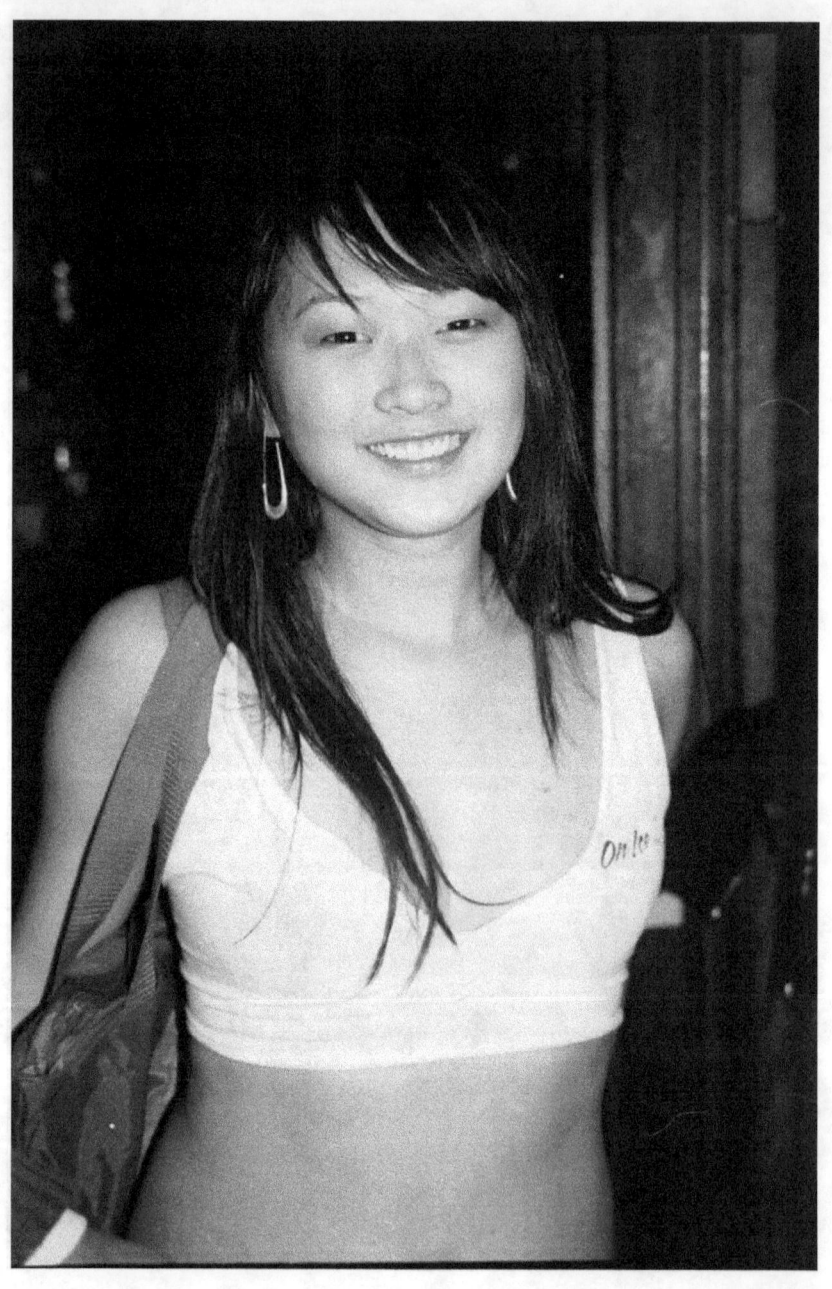

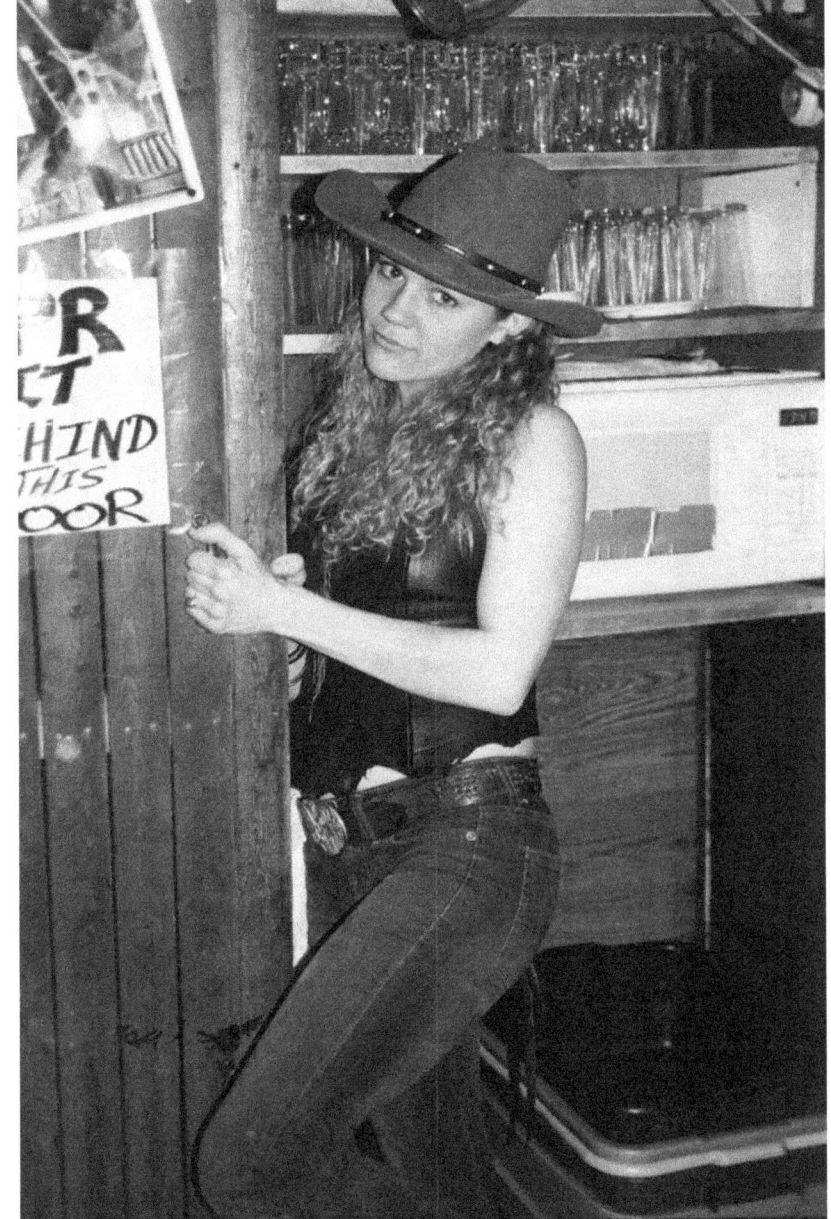

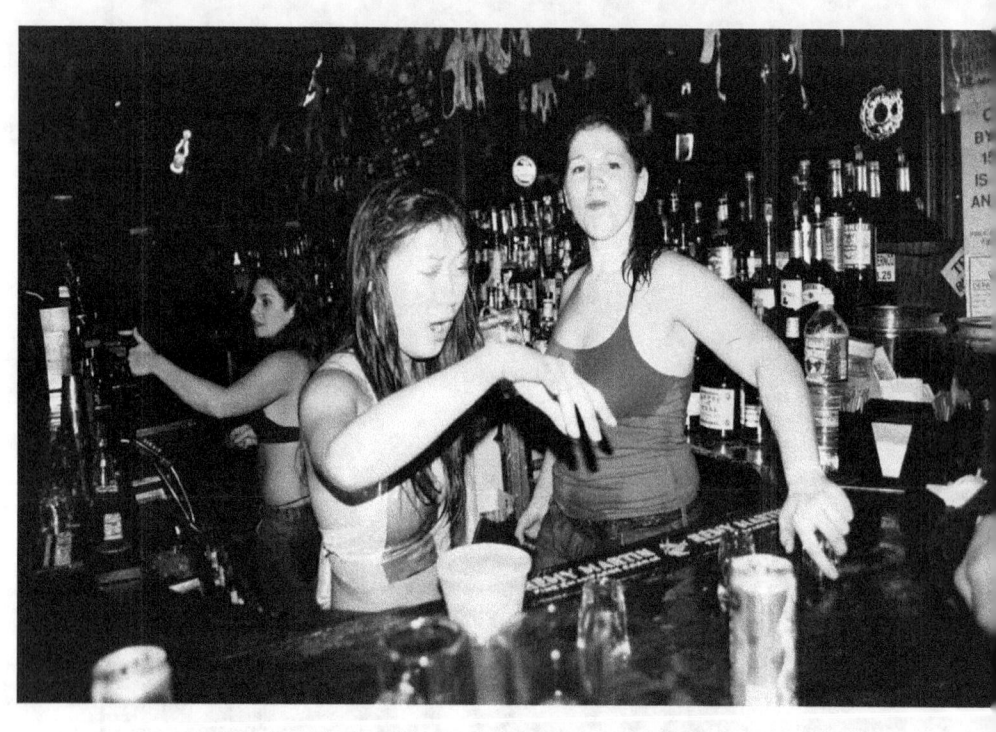

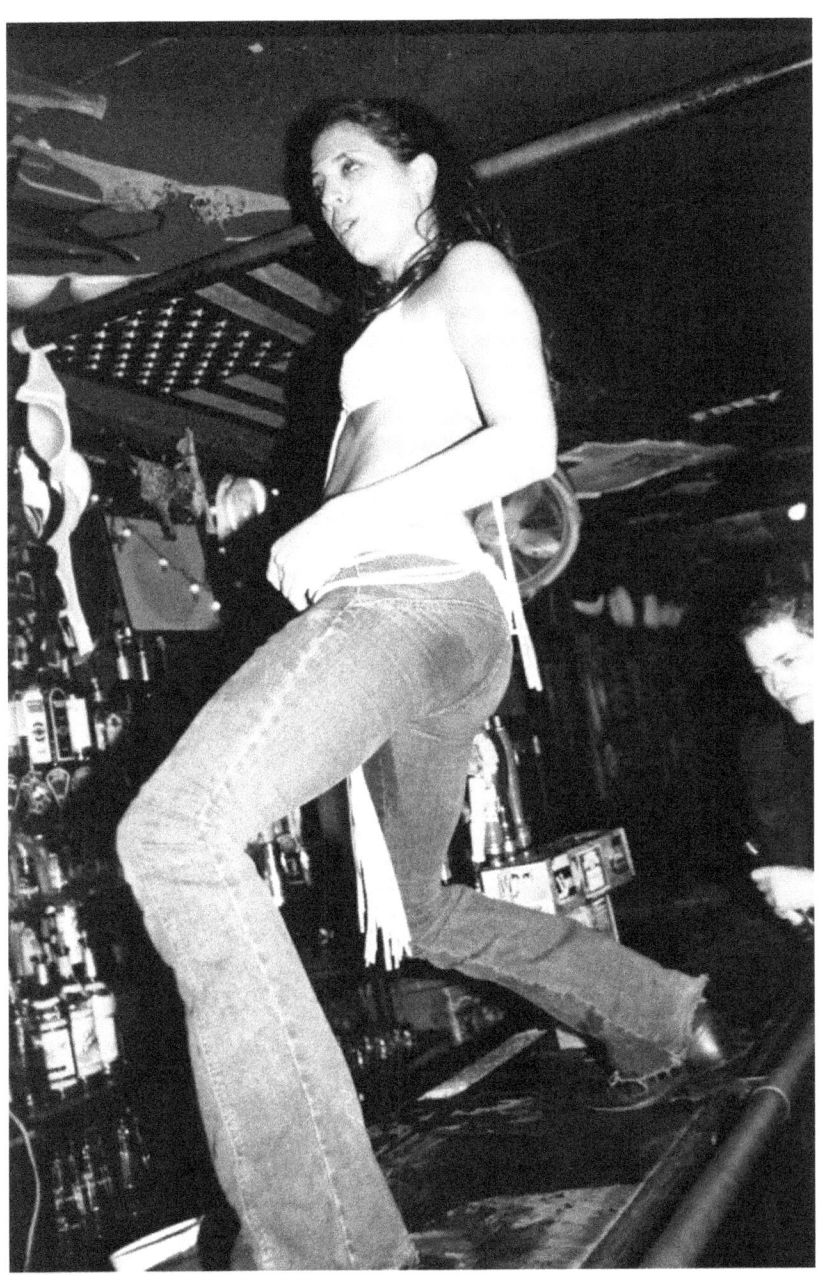

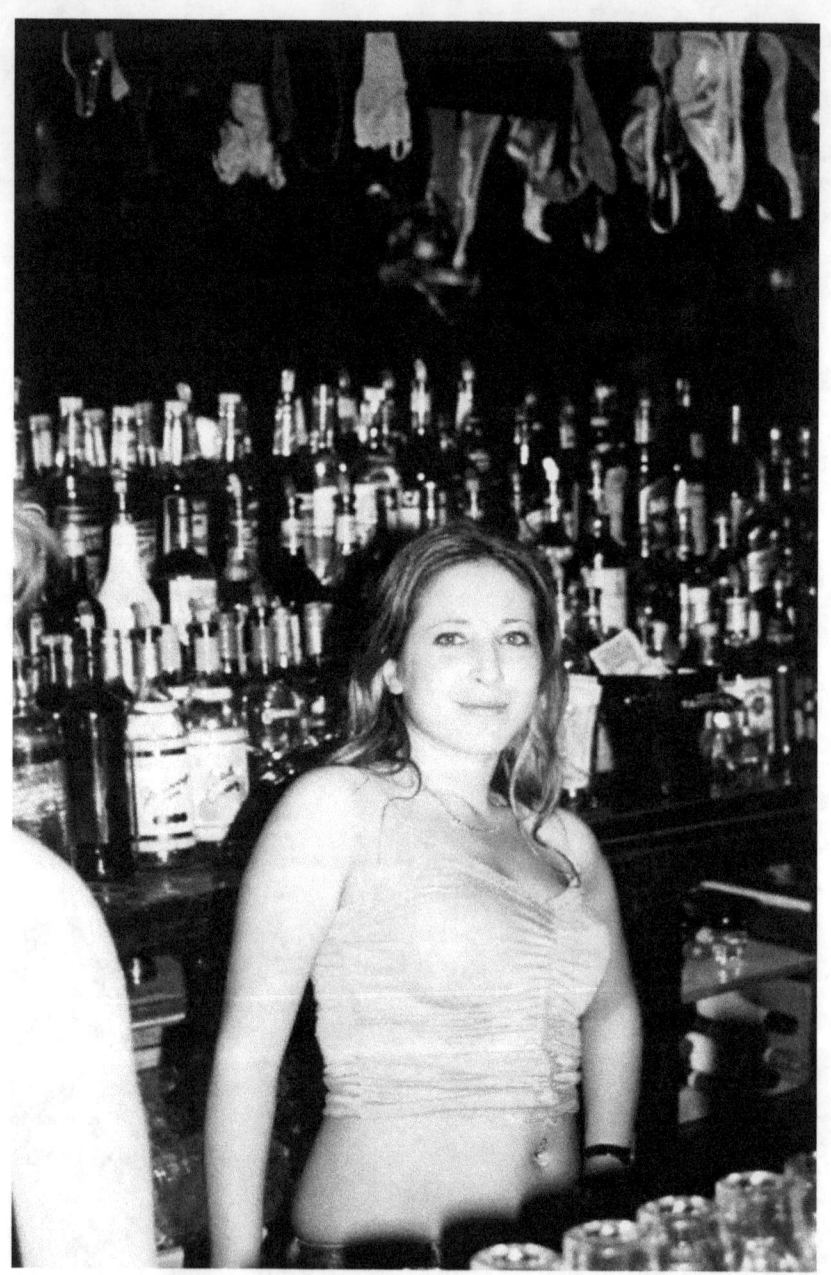

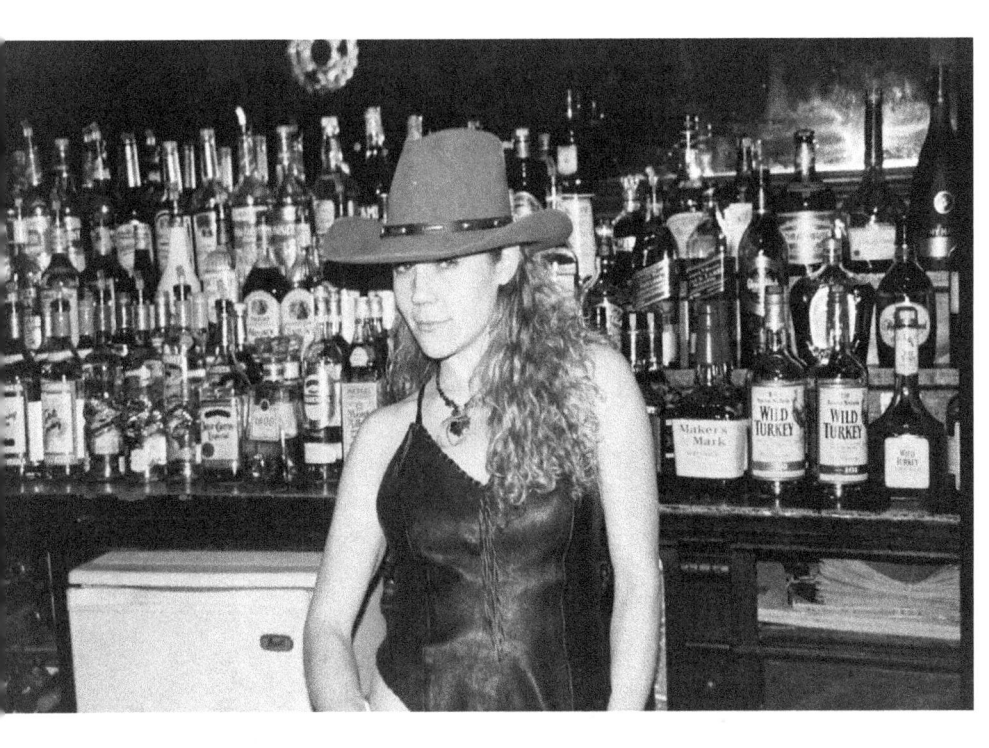

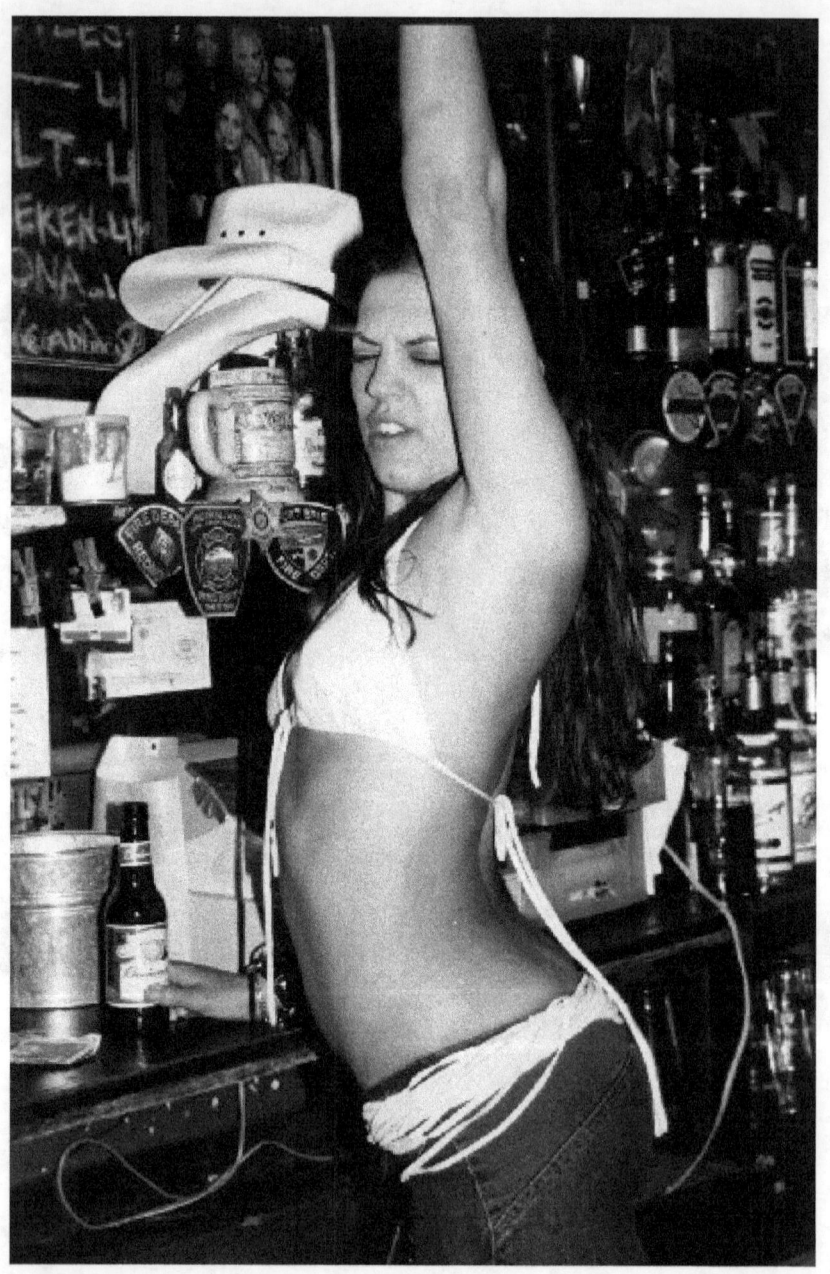

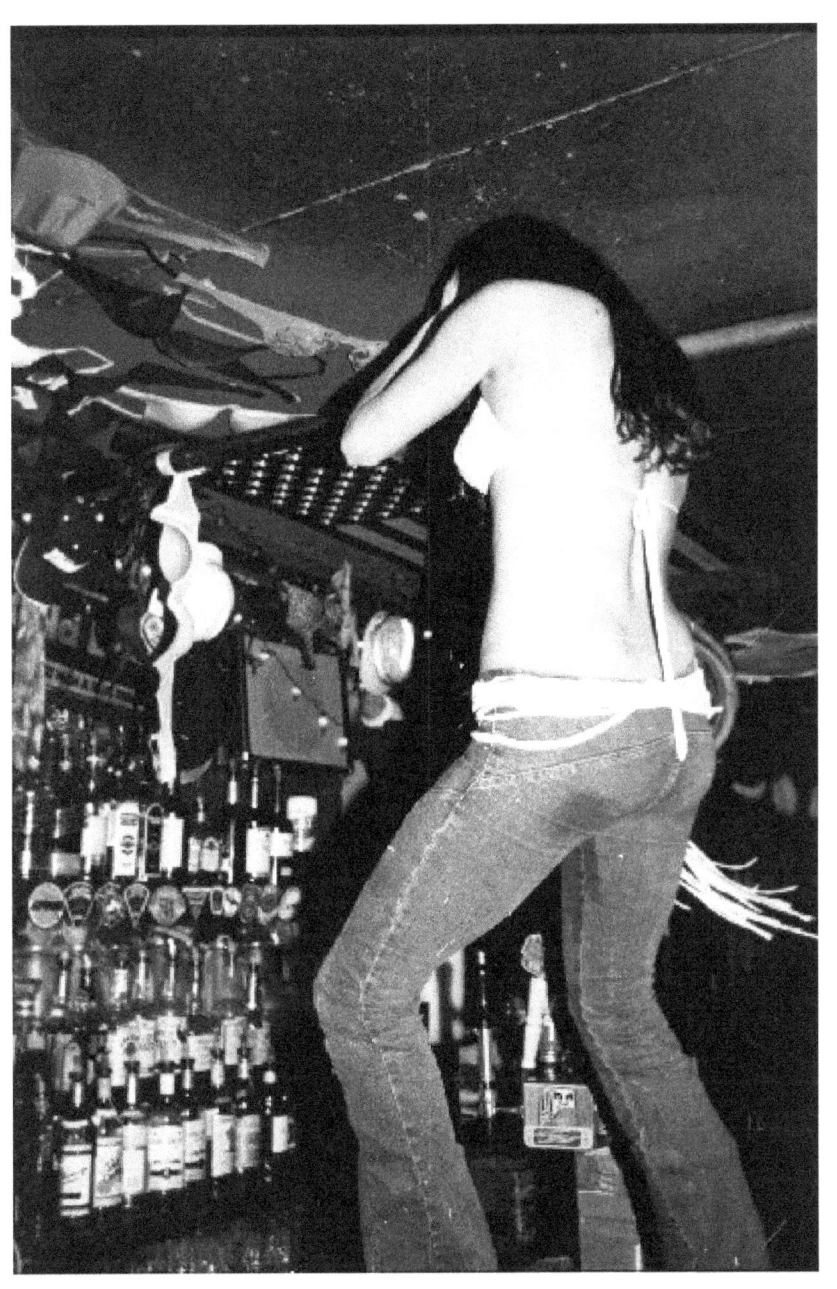

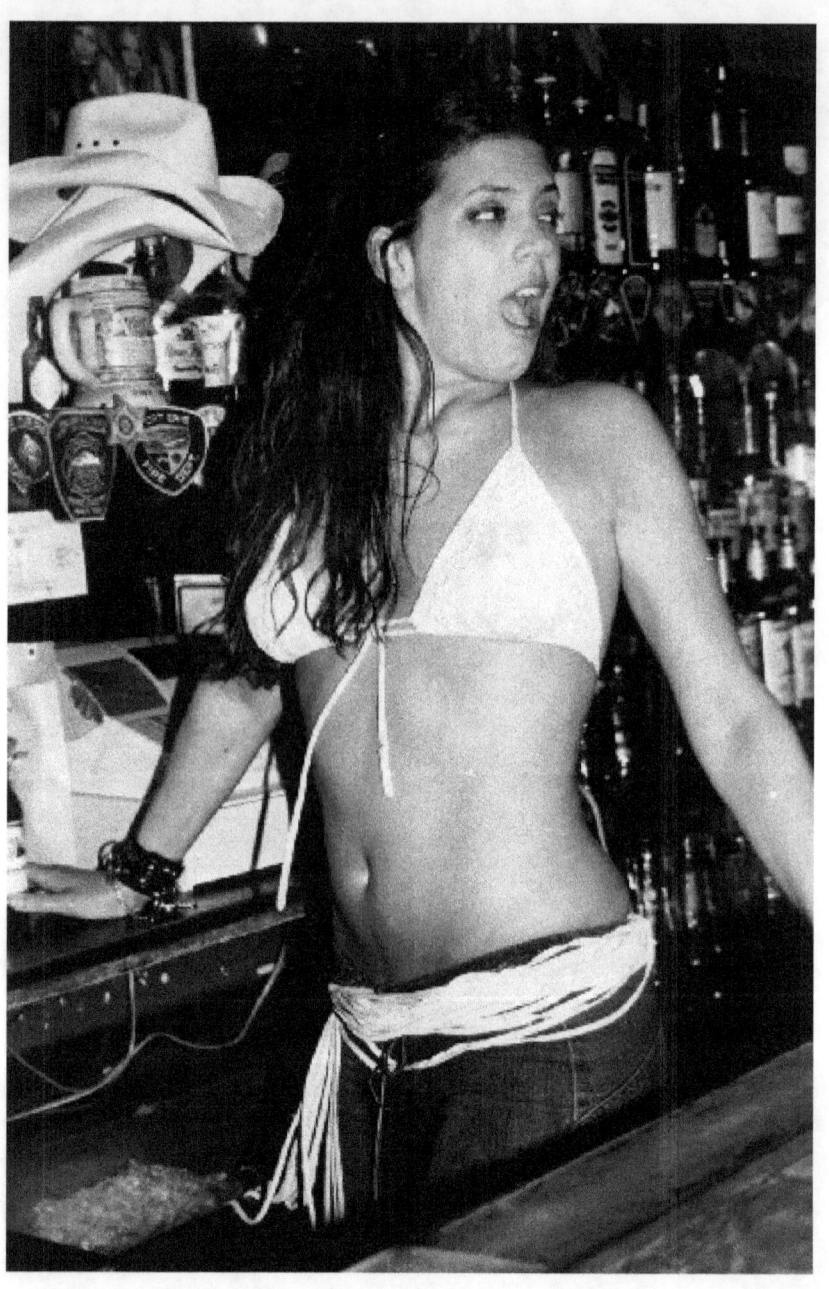

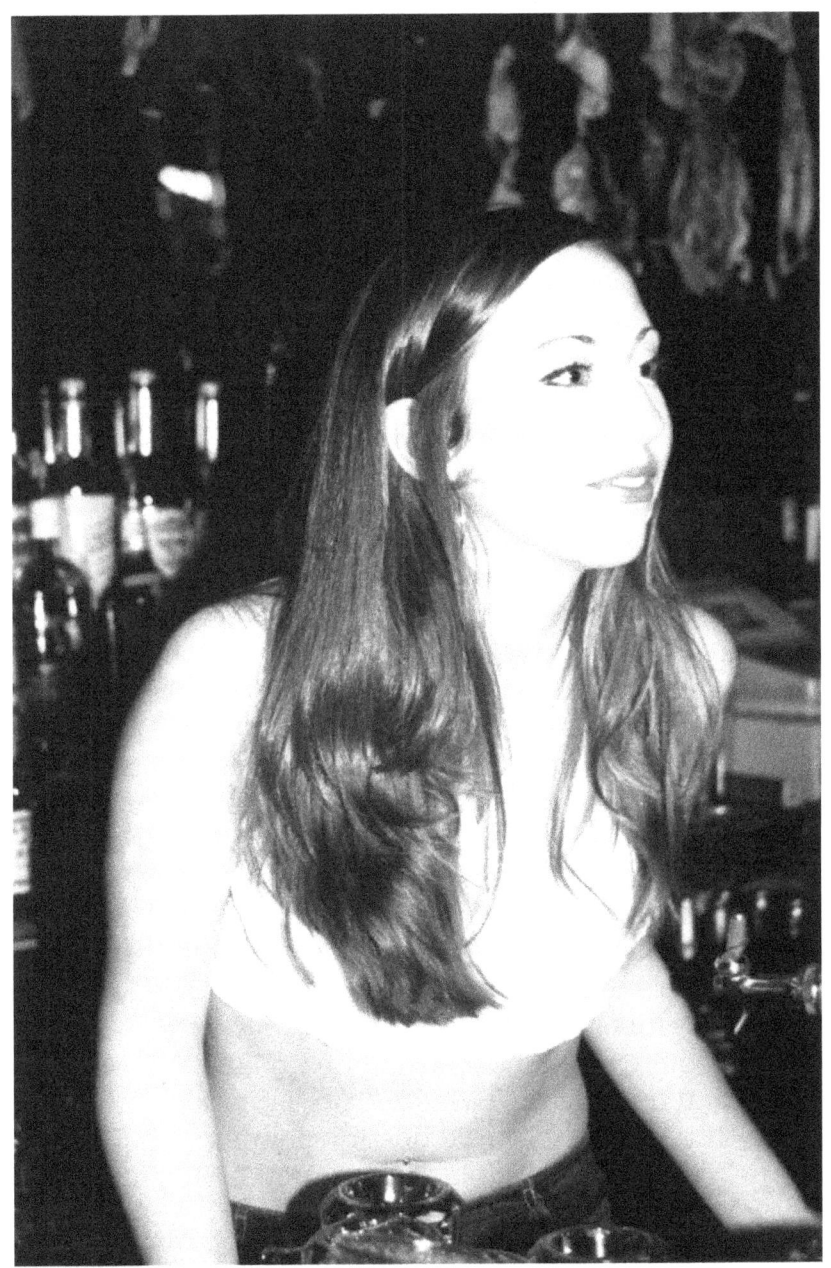

Drinking while Writing while Writing while Drinking: Part One: Abita Grapefruit IPA and Brennivin Schapps
03/05/2014

While listing my top ten New York City bars today, I am swigging Abita Grapefruit IPA (wonderful citrus notes with the right kind of funk) and sipping Brennivin Schnapps from Iceland (like Vicks vapor rub poured in cold gin equaling the medicine you don't need, but want). Over twenty years of late nights, early afternoons in drinking holes and saloons...these are the ten or so that put my liver back in a New York Groove...

10. The Baby Doll Lounge (defunct). Just below Canal Street lay this decrepit peeler joint with bathrooms as bad as the Mars Bar (honorable mention for this list). You can gleam the outside in the film version of the NY Post headline "Headless Body in Topless Bar" (yes, there is such a film, but the interiors were shot in LA). Nearby, semi-legal places like The Harmony Theater and Blue Angels offered soft touch dancing and potato chips, but The Baby Doll Lounge looked like the bar that Satan would own. The girls on stage could care less - I once watched a heavyset stripper spent her entire three song allotment picking something from her teeth. Somehow guys and drinkers kept coming back. The bud bottles were reasonably priced but one friend swore off the place when one sloped-face stripper mentioned, that despite her recent stroke, she could wink another body part. She did, and my friend ran from the bar. Sadly, The Baby Doll couldn't survive a Guilani run city and despite changing the neon sign from "Topless" to "Stopless" (much like Billy's did in Chelsea), the Baby Doll would become a high end Italian restaurant, forever altering the location's clam specials.

9. Red Rock West (defunct). On 17th street within view of the High Line is one of Manhattan's worst pizza places, but its former tenant use to bring such joy to sailors and bikers and the ladies who love the boys with crew cuts or long unruly hair. Red Rock West always had the largest bouncers and it was good to know the bouncers. Behind the bar, the all female staff wore very little and rock and roll blared at an incredible decibel level. The bartenders all had their tricks from breathing fire to pouring a whole beer bottle down her jeans (Kimmie - where are you now?). It was the place to be for Fleet Week and my long haired friend Dinshaw and I would dress in short order cook shirts, sailor hats, and say we were from the USS Titanic. Those get-ups helped the ladies distinguish us from the other clean cut sailors and we did better than one would imagine with such a cheap gimmick. I don't know why Red Rock West closed but the area has become a haven for Lindsey Lohan to be banned from bottle service clubs. It's too bad - Lindsey would have loved Red Rock, and the bouncers would have loved Lindsey.

8. The Corner Bistro. If this was a burger column, the Bistro would be #1. I insisted to the president of the Burger Club of America that the Corner Bistro was the best in the world and she asked, "If I was drunk when I was there." I was and am often, but it is still the best burger bar none. Every member of the the staff behind the bar are old souls and despite knowing where the bodies are buried, they will never tell. They will sell you the Bistro Burger, brimming with onion, lettuce, tomato and magical pickles, topped with bacon and dripping juice that is nectar of the Gods. And the fries are good too. I seem to only drink McSorely's when at the Bistro, but they have the goods at good prices. New York doesn't have the death penalty, but if it did, I guarantee the Bistro Burger would be the leading last meal on Death Row.

7. McSorely's. It claims to be the oldest bar in the US, but it also only let women in the 60s, Still, there is nothing pretentious about the sawdusted saloon. Everything historical is fading, but the beer - only light or dark served two at time - is as fresh as a Spring morning. Joseph Mitchell's words are now carried on by 40 year barman Geoffery Bartholomew and his poems. Watching the sun stream through the criss-crossed windows late afternoon onto the worn bar will turn one to poetry to describe the scene. The mustard is hot, the cheese plate is sliced cheddar and onions and a sleeve of Saltines, but the place has more charm than any four star hotel - McSorely's welcomes you back like a warm hug on a cold day. Light or Dark could describe men's souls just as well as your only choice at McSorely's, but I'll take the mugs over a moral compass any day or night.

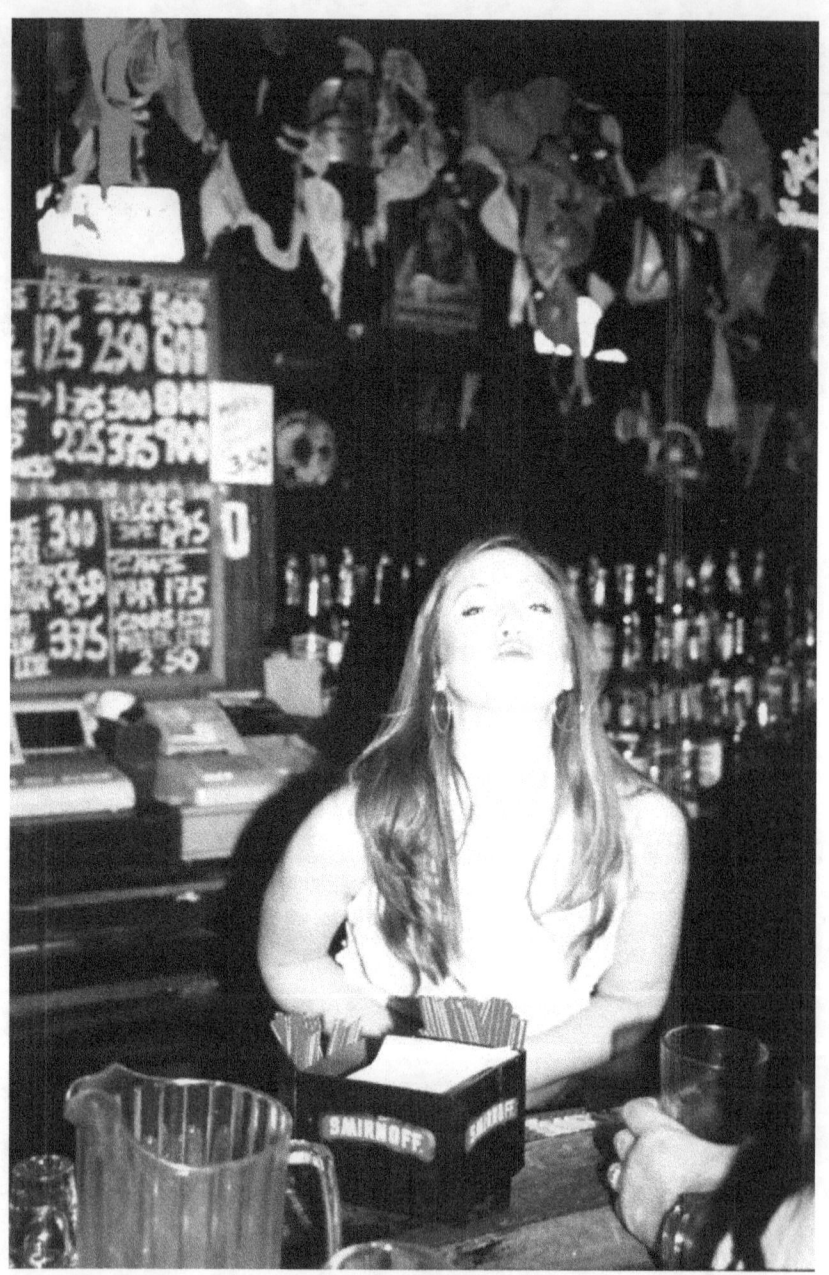

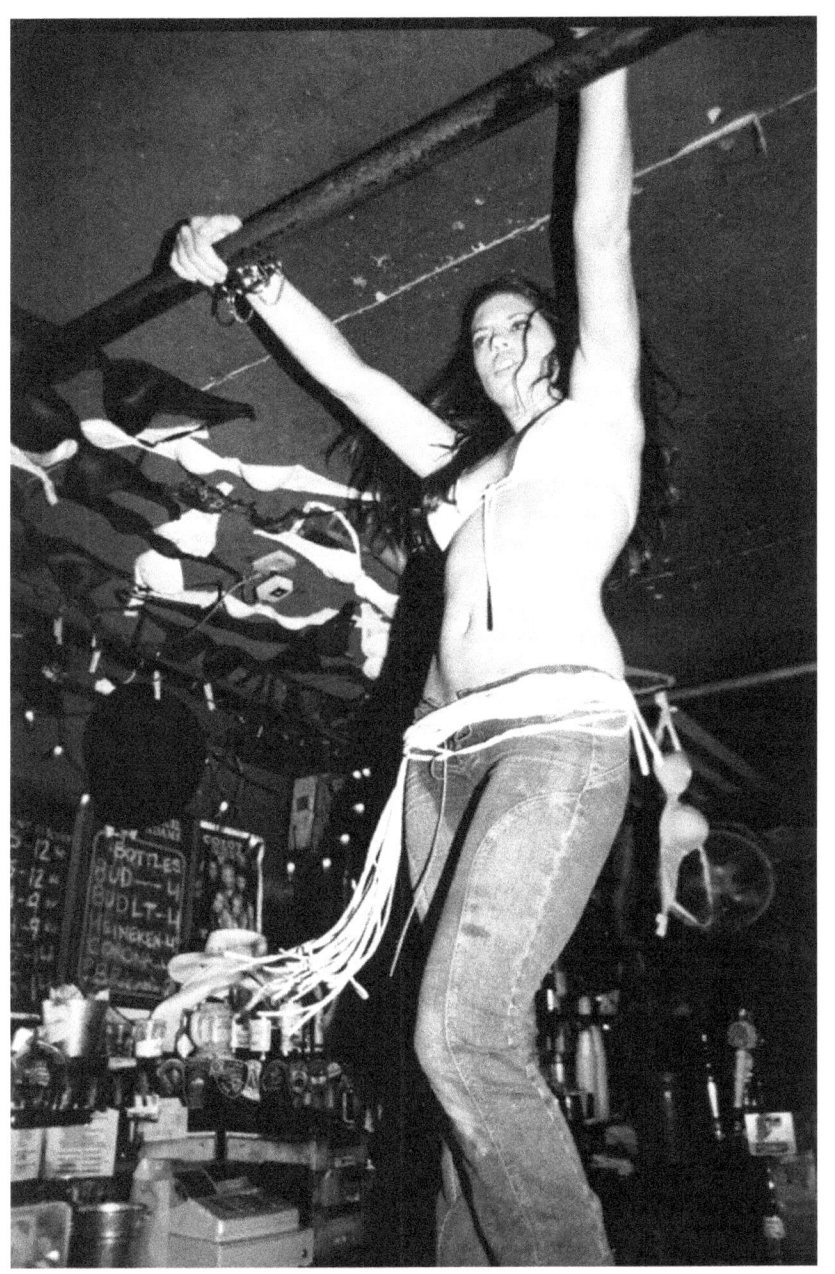

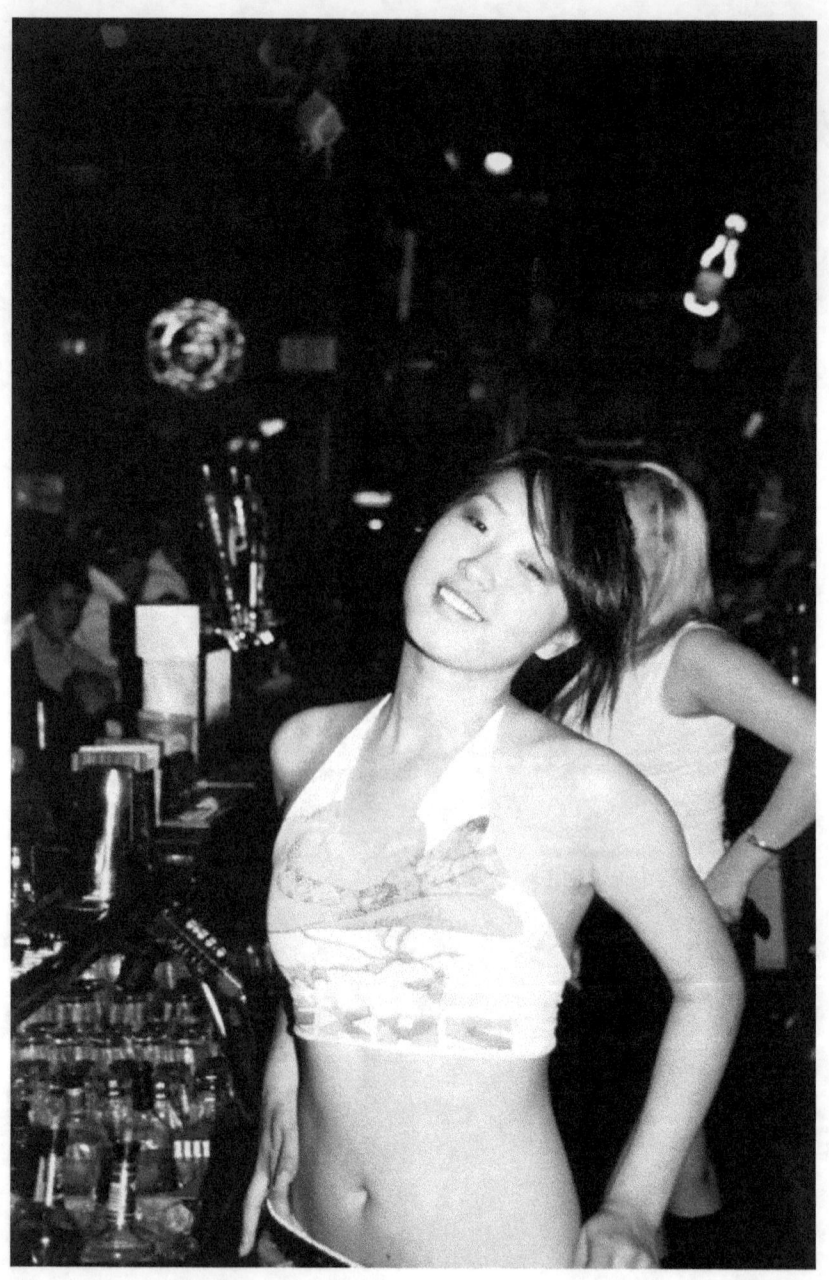

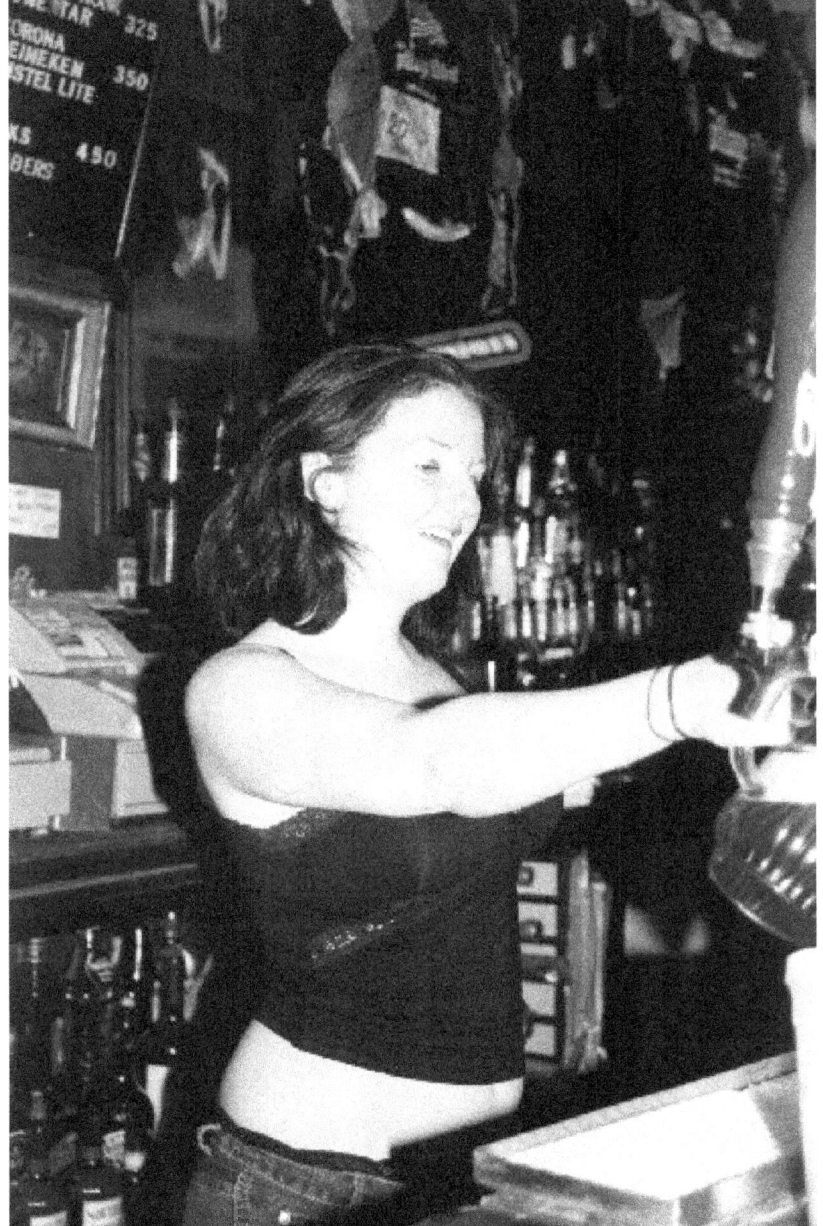

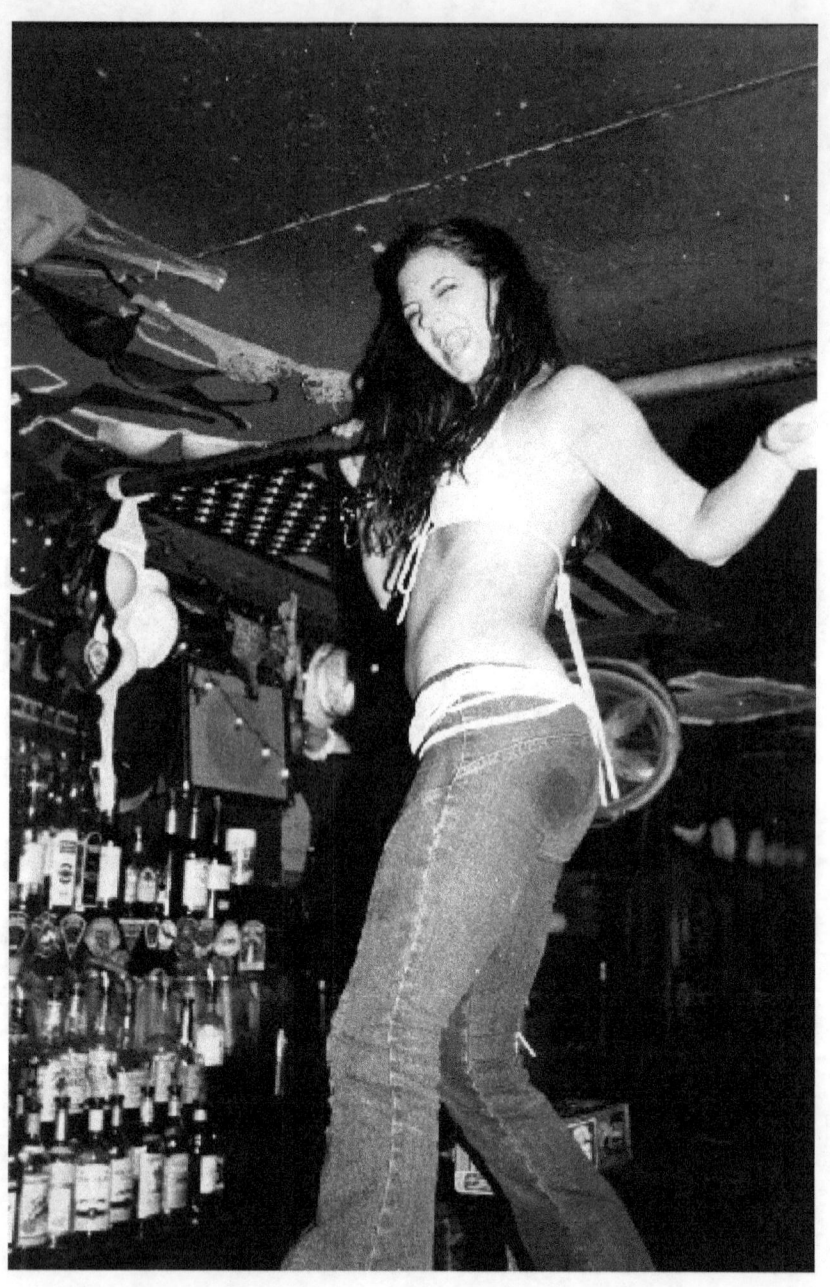

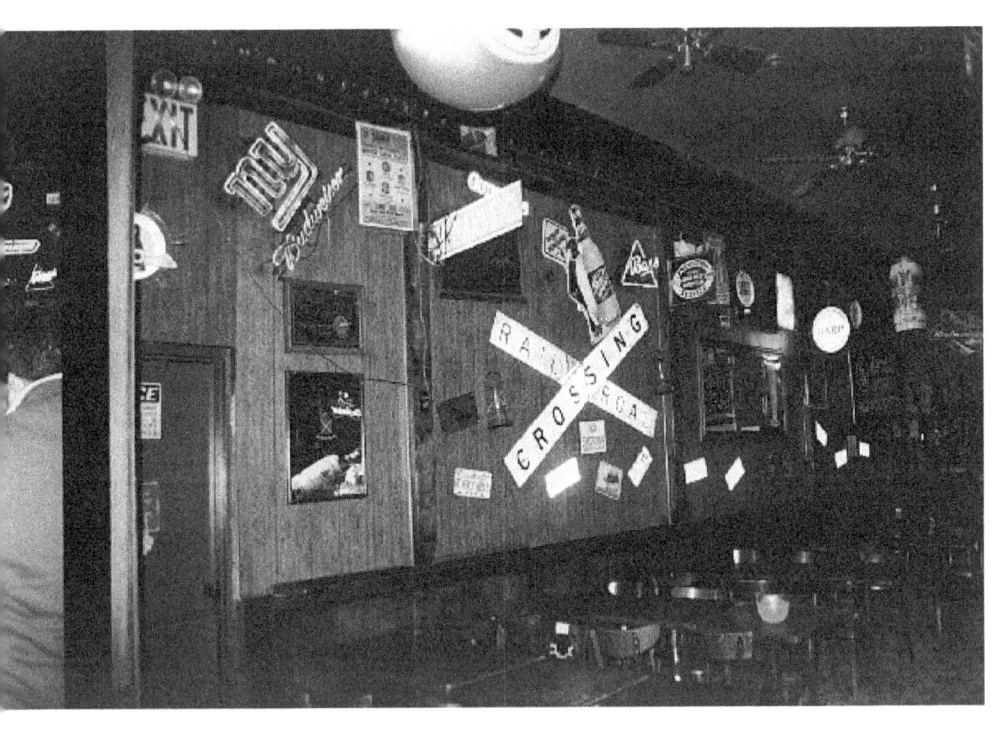

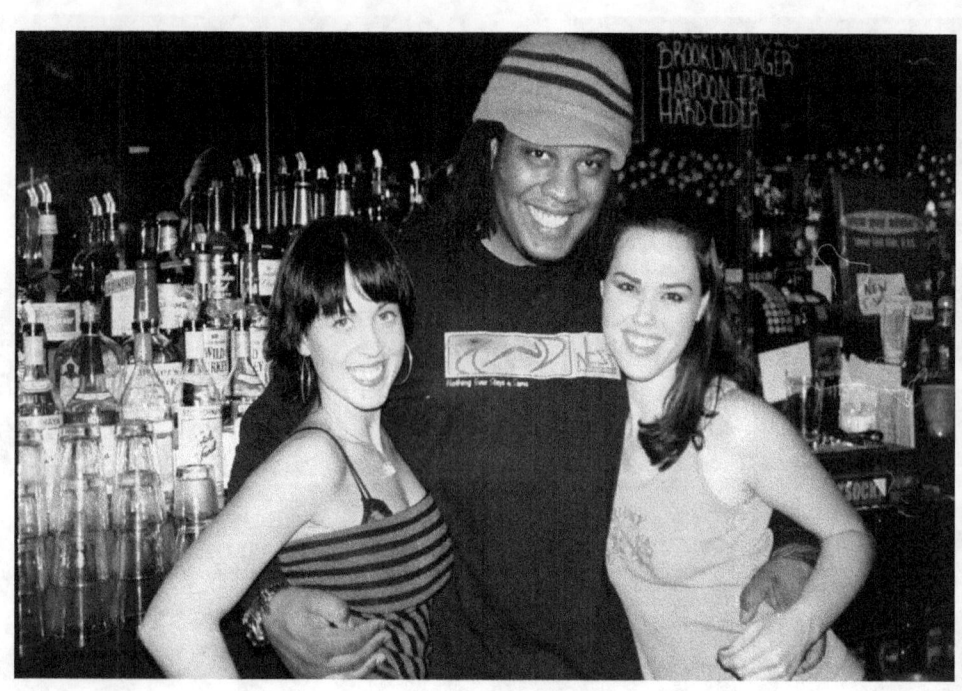

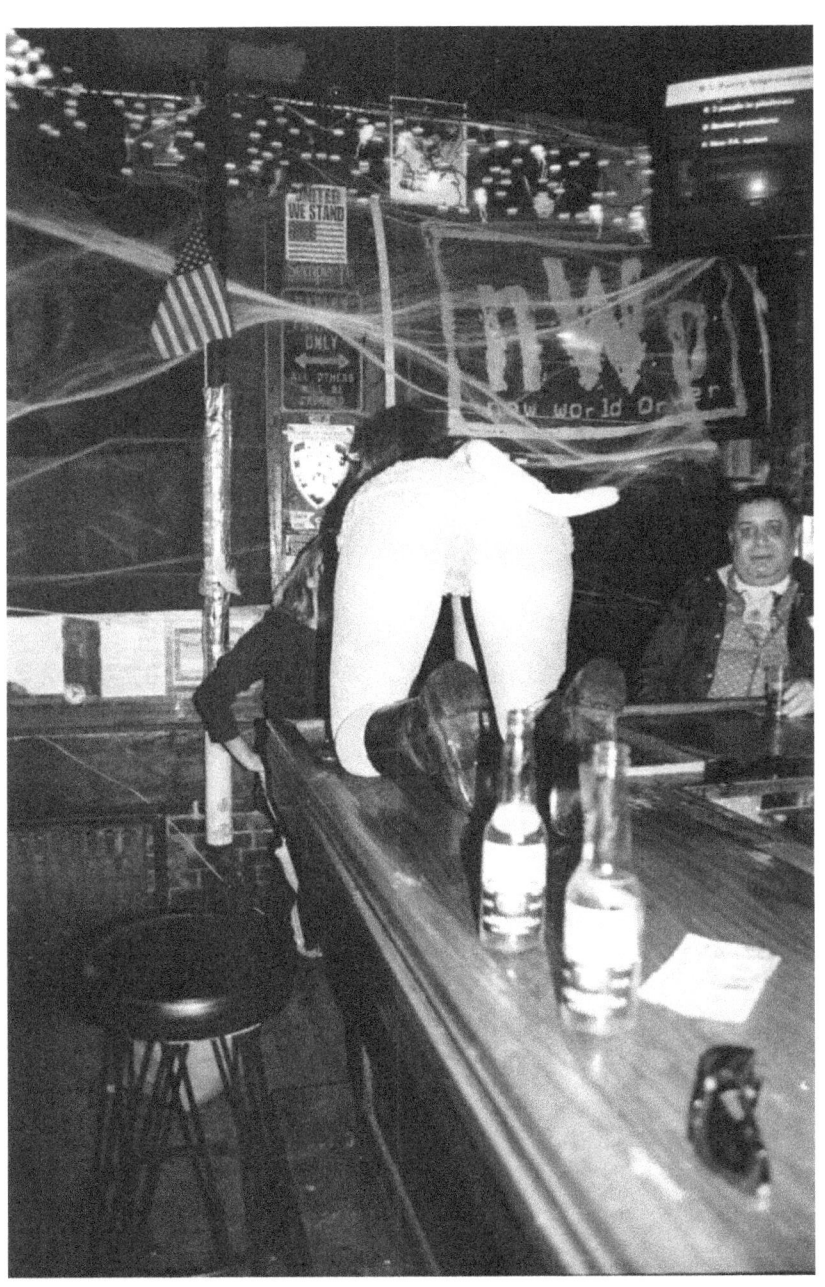

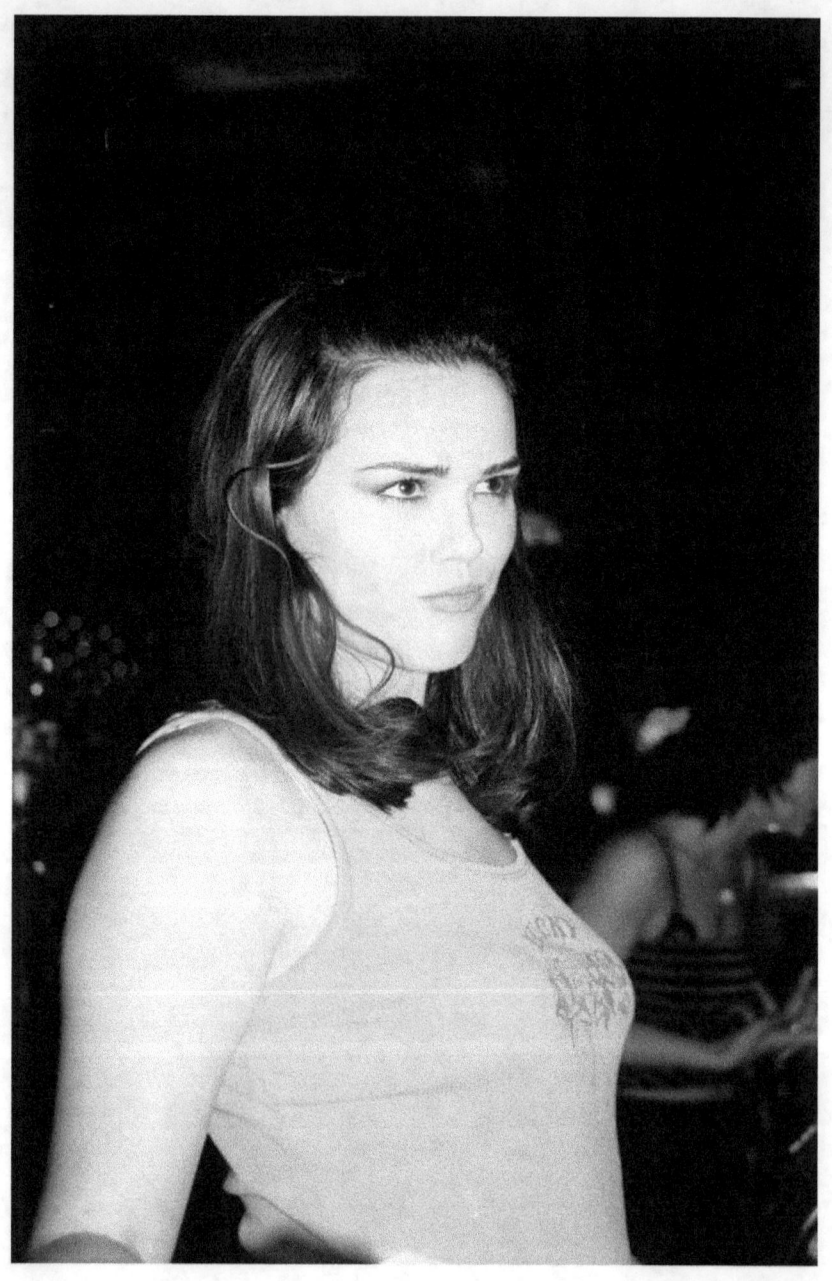

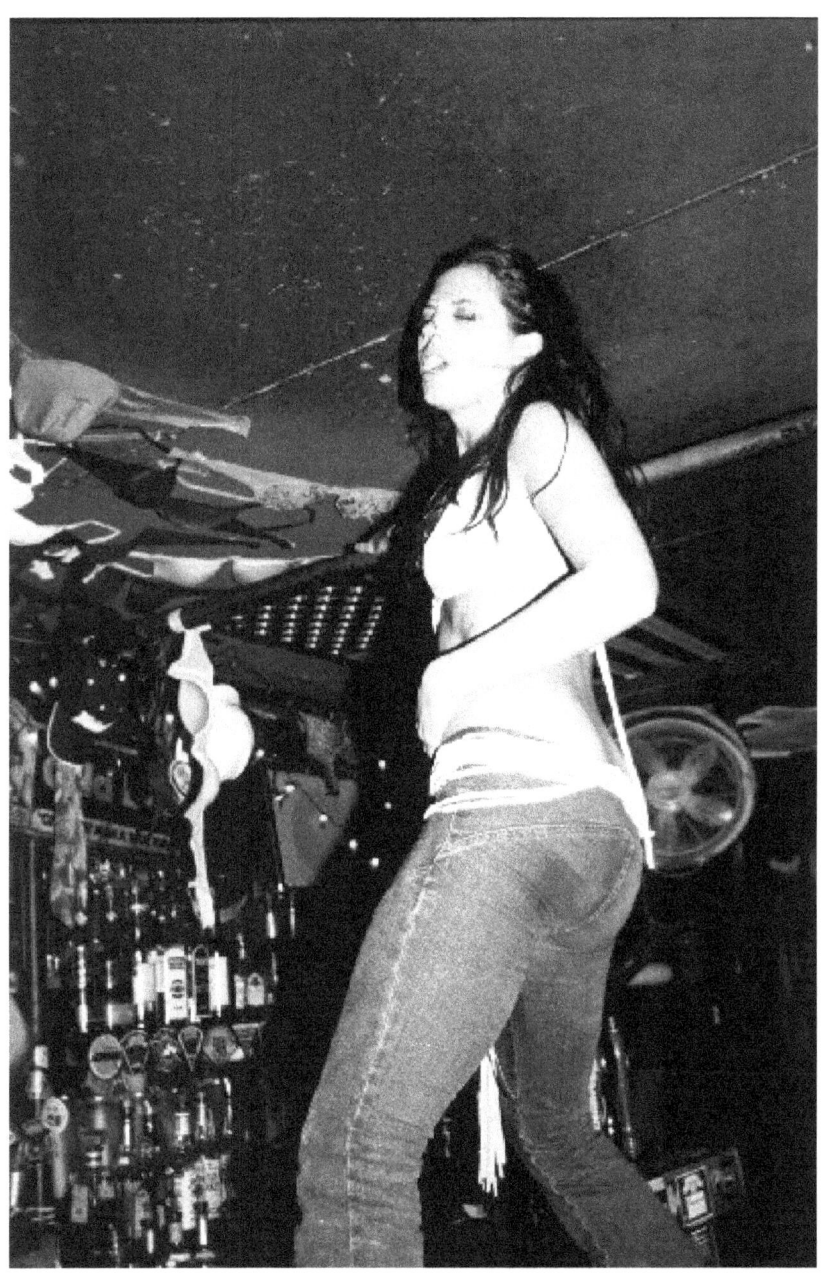

Drinking while Writing while Writing while Drinking: Part Two — Lagavulin 16-Year-Old Whiskey
03/06/2014

While still composing my ode to my favorite NYC dive bars, I am quaffing Lagavulin's 16-year-old whiskey from Islay. Some would use words like, "peaty" or "smoky" but for me this whiskey tastes like someone put a cigar out on a plate that had a pork slider on it and then dumped water onto it and collected the run-off. I consider that a compliment and the whiskey is wonderful from beginning to end.

6. Rudy's Bar and Grill. Did you say free hot dogs anytime you want...any amount you want? That would be enough to propel a bar to mythical standards, but several bars now offer free food. Rudy's is a throw back NYC bar — it's not Clinton when you are in Rudy's red duct taped booths — it's Hell's Kitchen. Rudy's opens at 8 am and there is usually a spirited discussion to go with the spirited liquid breakfast at that hour. One morning, the rummies and I couldn't figure out what movie was on the television — it was a western with a breathtaking Sophie Loren and then there was Burt Reynolds and suddenly Jim Brown — it was as if the drunks had remote controlled the casting. Sadly, it was not drunken hallucinations, but a 1969 film titled, "100 Rifles." I still like to think that the Rudy's morning crew willed the movie to happen, like a Choose your own Adventure book. Rudy's is the Old West and also the best place to hook up with the opposite sex at 3 am. It's true — the big pig outside is an aphrodisiac mascot calling out to all those who don't want to go home to their own beds...or livers.

5. Coyote Ugly. At the recent twentieth anniversary of the original dive bar the owner Lil, a stunning brown haired

beauty, thanked me for coming to her bar for twenty years. Really, I should have been thanking her and I as pointed to the returning revue of former bartenders, I told her as much. Kristy was there, but not Maria, my two favorites who gamely donned hot dog bikinis and burger bras and entered my shower for a DVD extra of the documentary about my competitive eating. Needless to say, it is a very popular DVD extra. Coyote Ugly, long before the franchised bar — over twenty "faux" dive bars in many cities and the article by Elizabeth Gilbert that turned into a movie (Why is her book not titled, "Drink, Pay, Lust?") — this bar was the real deal. I've spent six Thanksgivings in this bar. Granted, the regulars now are a collection that makes the crew from "One Flew Over the Cuckoo's Nest" look like Wall Street bankers, but occasionally the bar top is filled by girls shaking their booties and the juke box gets turned up to eleven. Lil's vision exists in the photos that adorn the walls and the bras that line the walls — Coyote Ugly, the original bar is a place to let it all hang out. I am often there and despite loving canned beer have drunk my lifetime quota of PBR. I'll take something in a bottle and if Anna, Christina, or Maya is pouring (or either of the stunning managers Danielle and Tahnee) then I will be at my bar seat for a long while. It is easy to knock this bar as a tourist trap, but if those walls could talk...well, they would slur. A lot.

4. Coopers (also Dempsey's). I walk out my door. I usually head to 2nd avenue. Perhaps that is why the Irish bar Dempsey's is my regular as opposed to The Edge at the end of my block (Sebastian Junger preferred The Edge but he's a lot tougher than me and gets paid for his writing). Dempsey's is a real Irish bar, where the person tending bar and the girl running food are from Ireland. I would love to start a Youtube channel titled, "Fake Irish Bars Around the World," because I've been in a lot of them from Singapore to Thailand (although there is a good one in Guam). The Irish Fry Up is great, the Guinness is

poured slow, and the Shepard's Pie will both cure and cause a hangover depending on one's mood and accompanying beverage. Dempsey's is owned by a neighborhood bloke named Tom, who feels that if the East Village is good enough to raise a family in, then it's good enough to welcome the regulars to a second bar. Taking a location that was cursed since the diner moved across the street, Tom opened Cooper's. It has big beautiful windows so one can see the equally big beautiful beer boards. I prefer Cooper's over The Pony Bar or Tiger Ale House, all NYC gourmet beer bars. The beers rotate like a George R. R. Martin plot and it's best to not to become too attached to a characteristic brew, because it will be gone soon, but another worthy pour will take its place. The Scotch egg is the best I have had and the wings look as if the chickens competed in the Olympics before getting fried and sauced. Cooper's is a day drinker's destiny and the bar can support one's frame as one bounces from hoppy ales to strong stouts. It is the only bar that I don't order a beer — I ask the bartender to chose for me. I have never been disappointed. Slainte... which I assume is Irish for, "pour me another."

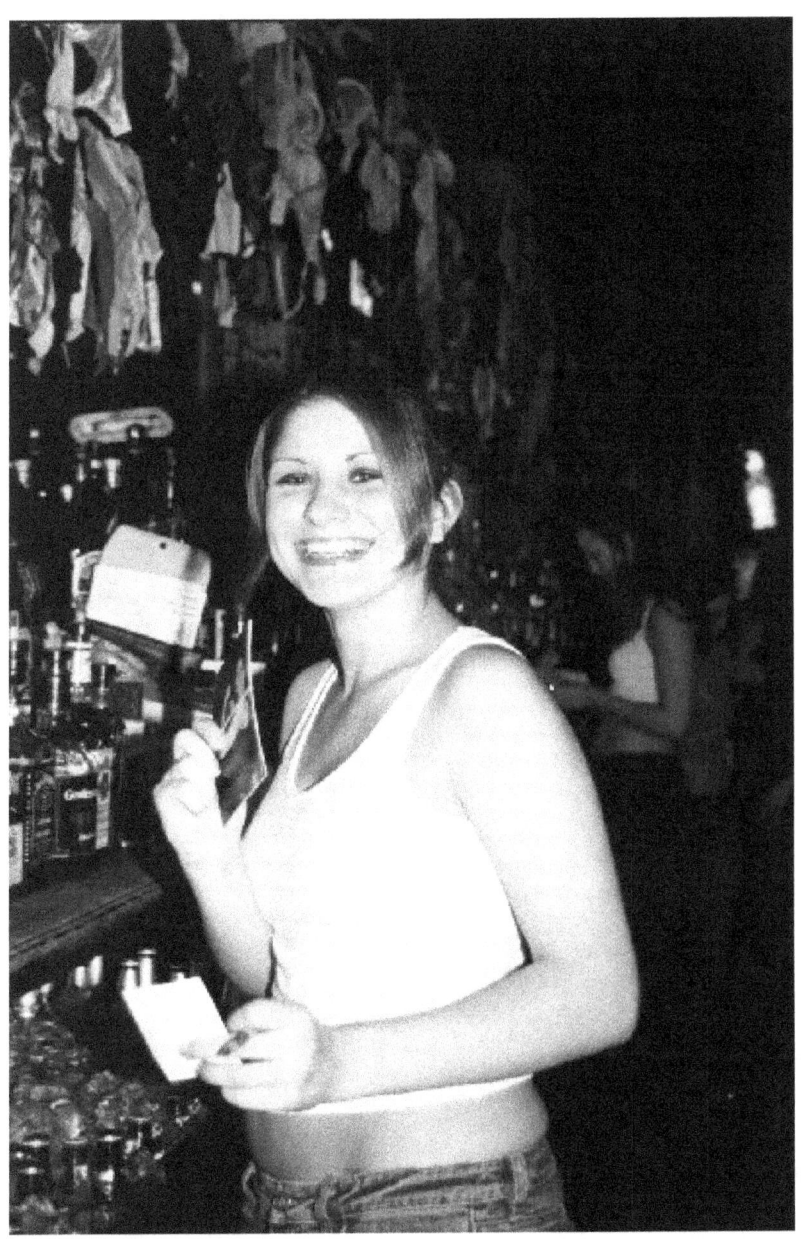

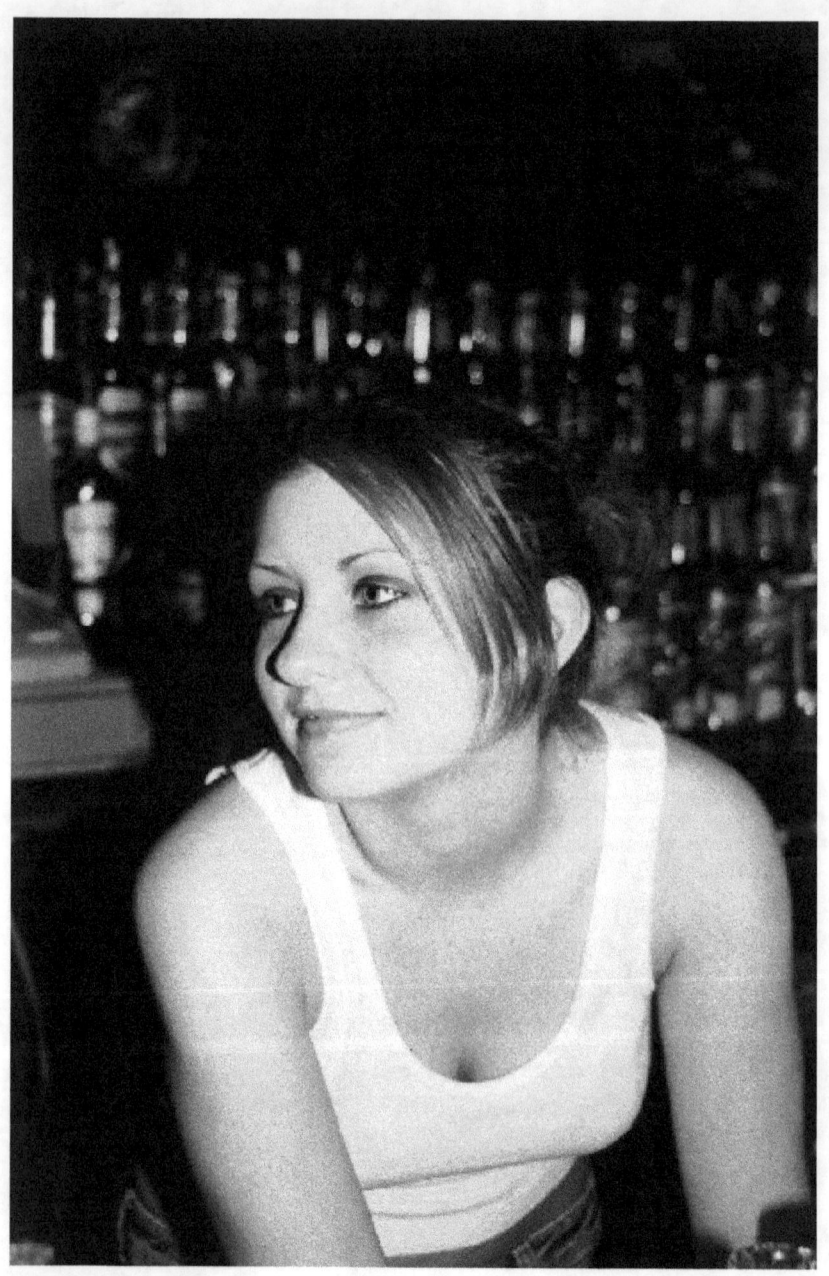

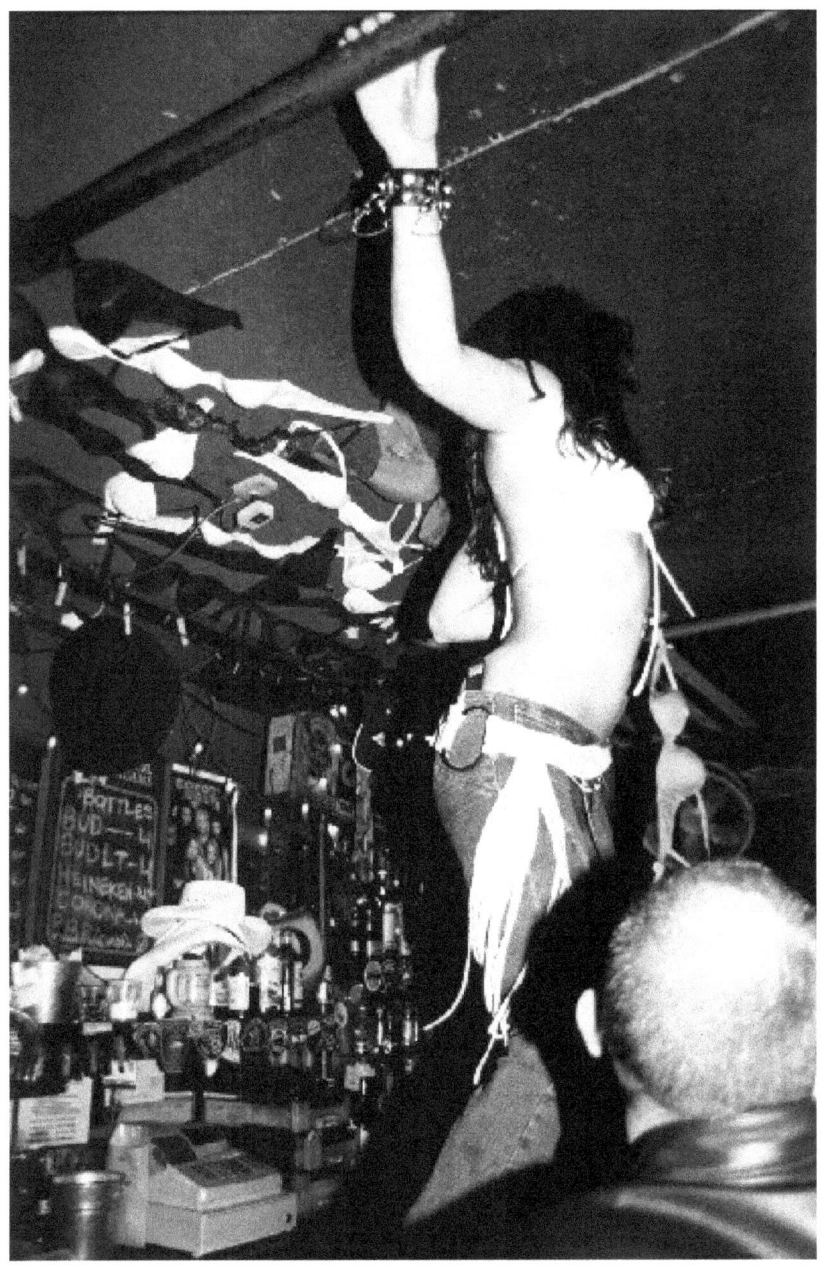

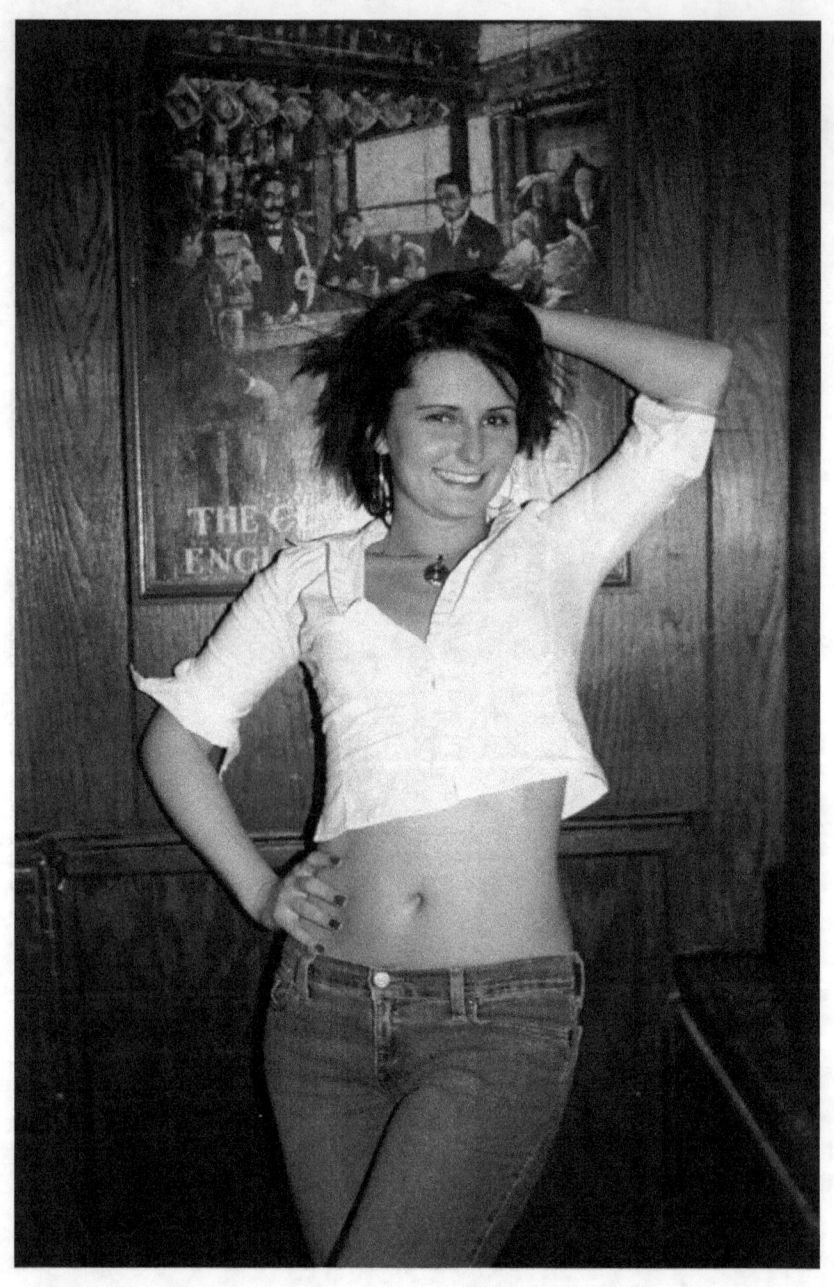

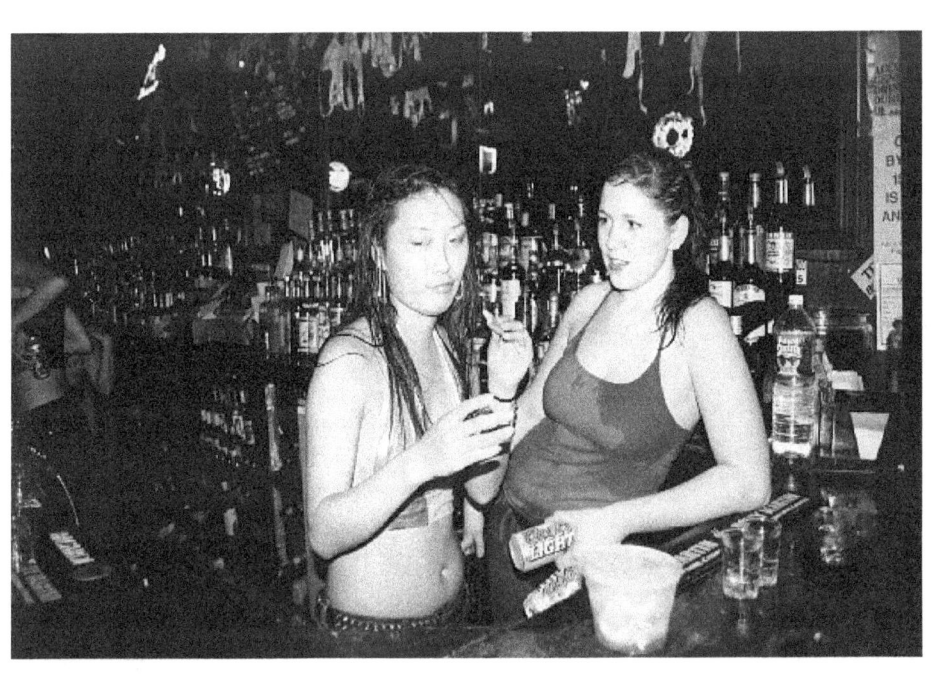

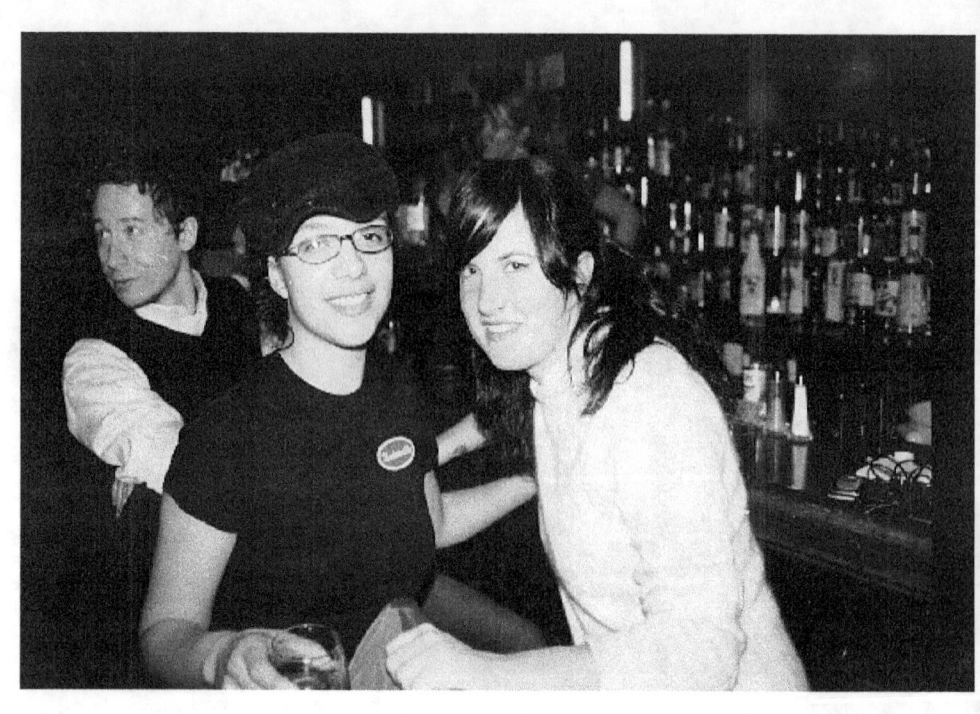

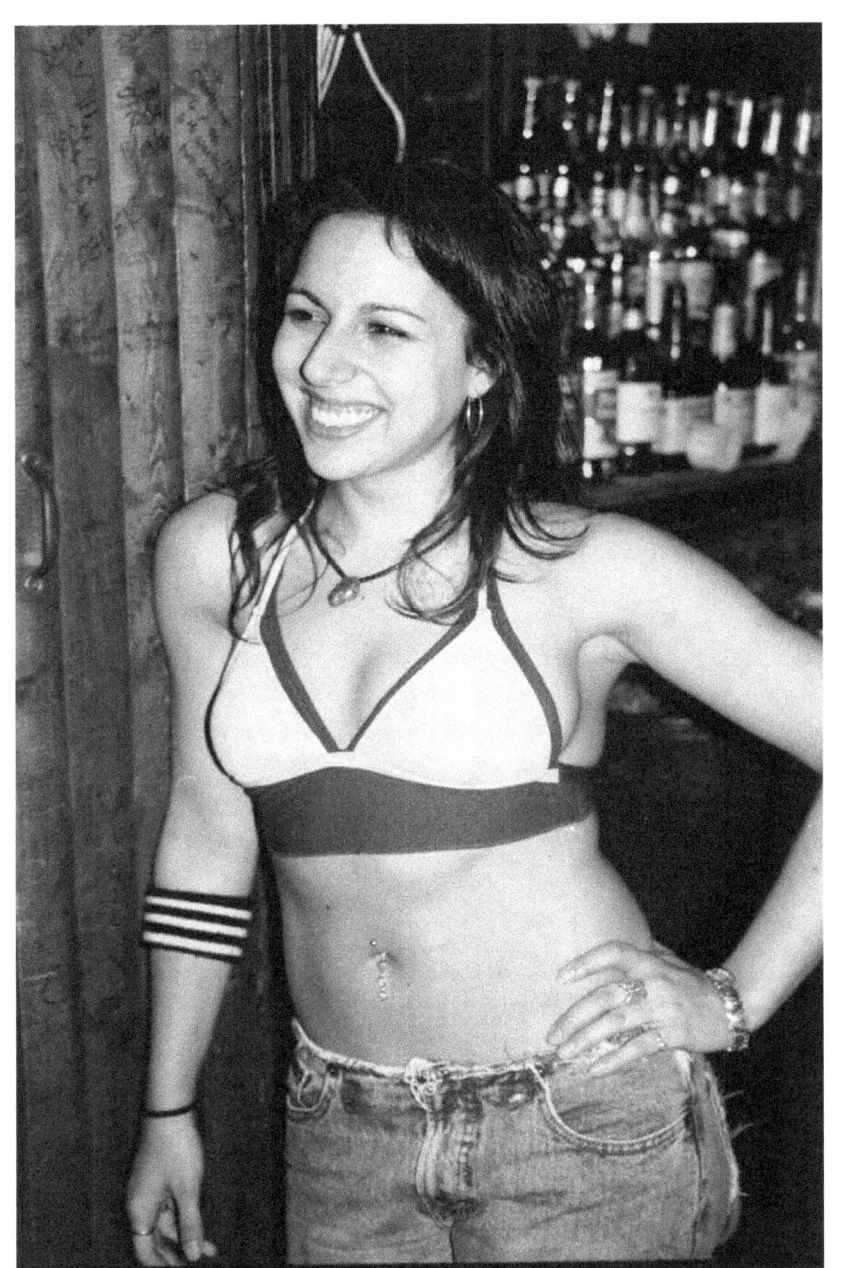

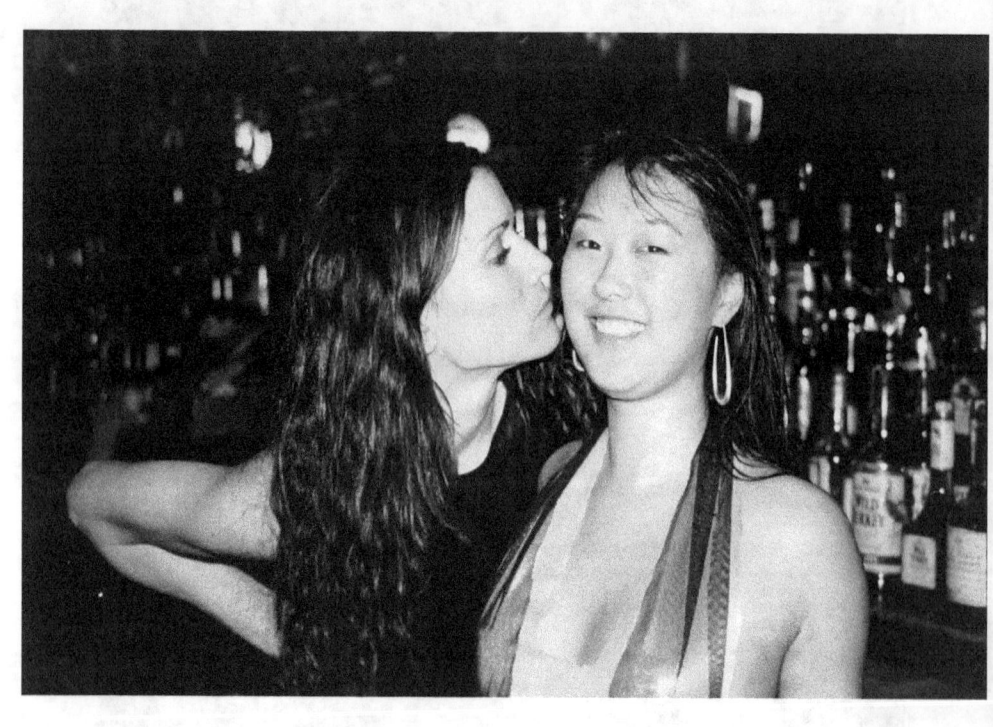

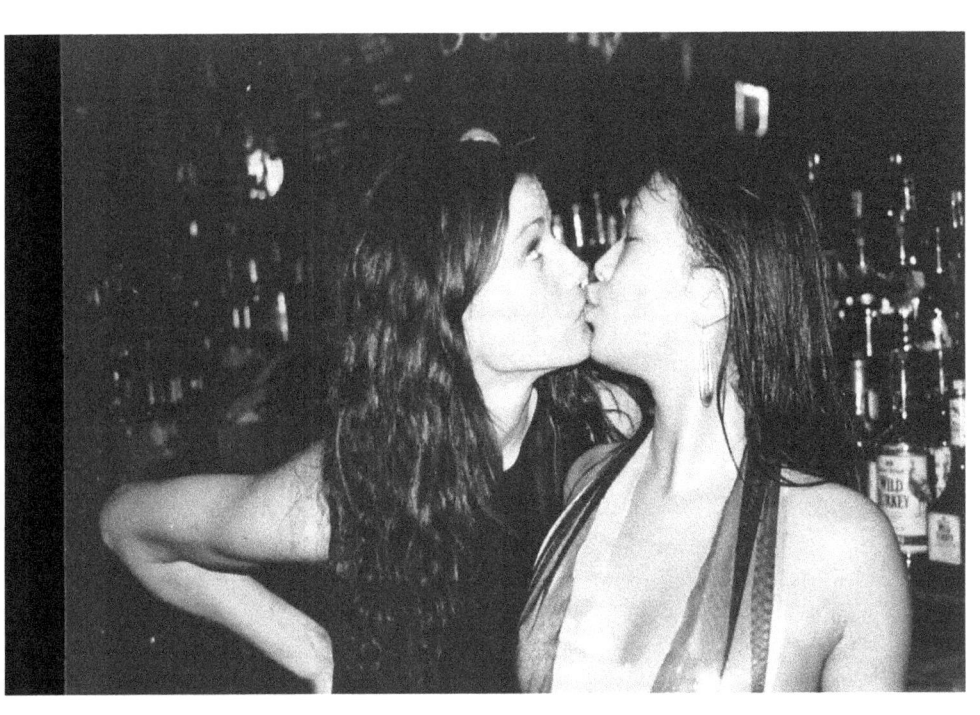

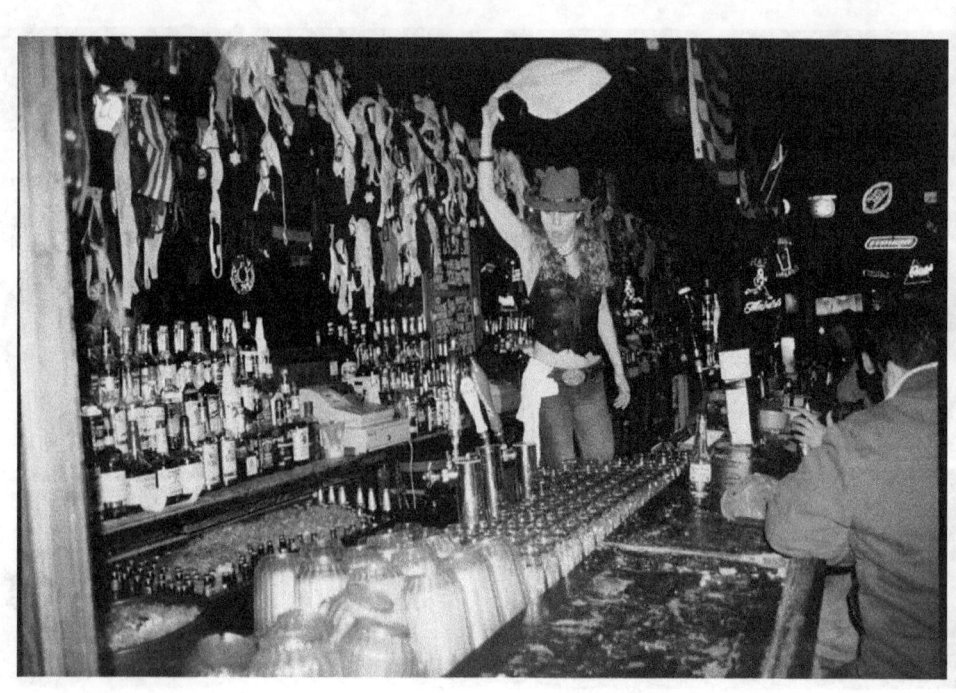

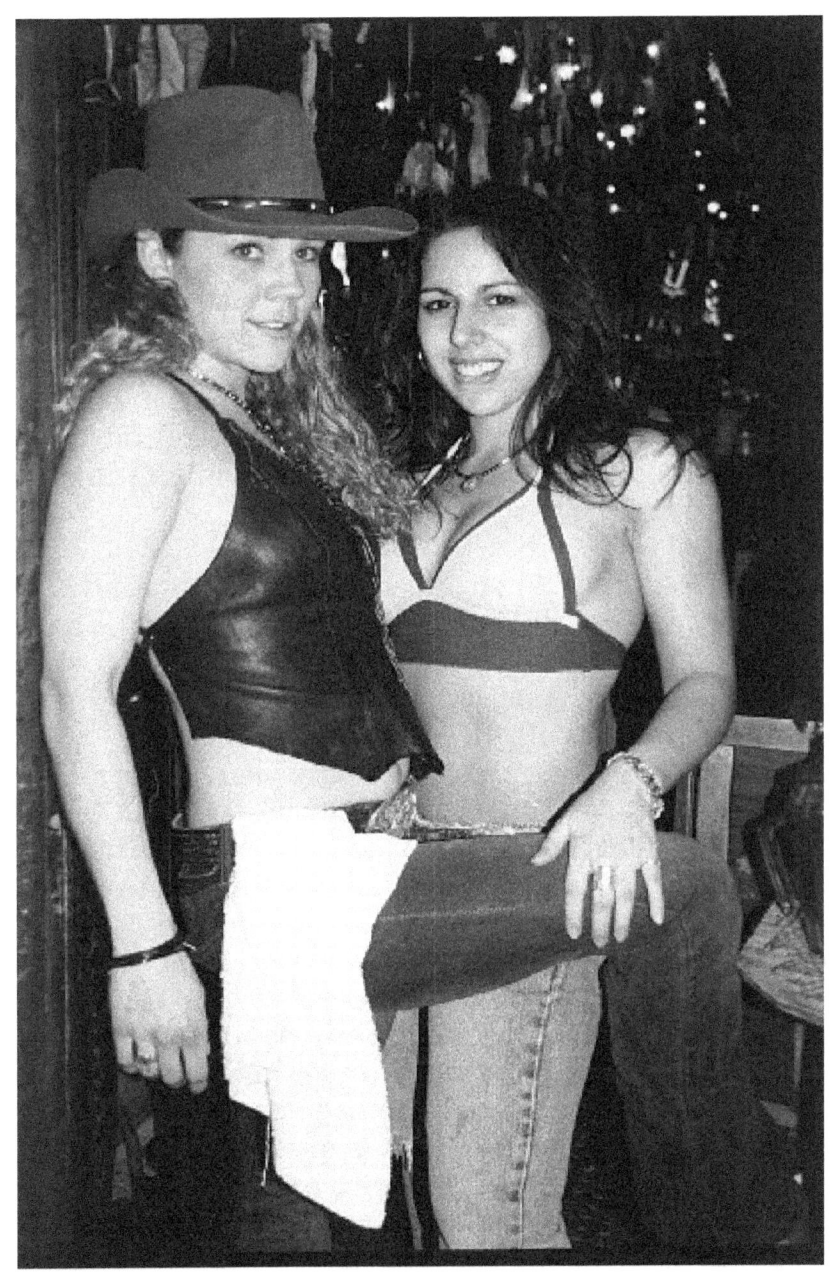

Drinking while writing while Writing while Drinking: Part Three — National Bohemian 'Natty Boh' Canned beer
04/02/2014

The final installment of my favorite dive bars in NYC has me drinking my all time favorite beer — Natty Boh from Baltimore. In a twist on "Smokey and the Bandit," I drive the drink up from Charm City as often as I can. The B'-More grit is washed away and the metallic tint of the can helps the taste of this fine beer. In the Canton neighborhood, Nacho Mama's serves Natty Boh in bottles and in the rare 40 oz bottle. Those 40 oz are like drinking an endangered species. On to the final three bars...

3. Hogs and Heifers — When I first went to this bar in 1993 there was a Polaroid of Charles Bukowski at the bar, hanging on the back wall by a thumb tack. It stayed for many years until someone stole it and left the tack (Note: It might not have actually been Bukowski, but I can drunkenly dream.) Over the last twenty years, everything — the plastic marlin, the motorcycle, the 10,000 bras, have been covered in a dust so thick, that the outside circumference of the ceiling fan has stalagcites of dust hanging down. Change comes slowly, if at all. When Coyote Ugly became the movie tie in Mecca, Hogs and Heifers went with a "Dick's Last Resort" style of service to compensate. It didn't last long, because the truth is that the bartenders are naturally tough (also beautiful) and if they are rude to customers they generally have good reason. Hogs and Heifers was a dive when the Meatpacking Neighborhood was filled with only blood-stained labcoat wearing meatpackers and negligee wearing transvestite hookers. It has stayed a dive while today the neighborhood is besieged by high-end fashion, twenty dollar martinis, and a price increase at Hector's, the remain-

ing diner. There are two rules as you enter — no gang colors and no ties (they will be cut off by the bartender). There is a third unspoken rule — no bullshit. Basically, Hogs and Heifers has zero tolerance for bullshit despite the onslaught of tottering high heels on the cobblestones, folded sweaters, and bottle service. It's true in the age of cellphones, rarely does some drunken cutie get up on the bar and bare her breasts, but the beer costs the same and the music is just as loud. I think if Marty McFly was going to appear in a fourth film — he would find himself at Hogs and Heifers — the only place in NYC where one can go back to the future. Still, I wish someone would return that Bukowski Polaroid.

2. Professor Thom's — I consider the greatest sports bar in America to be Cole's in Buffalo. It has what is needed — old trophies whose victories were discontinued in the 70s, beer ads from a different time, and walls that have captured the cheers and tears of generations of sports fans. Professor Thom's is a Boston bar in NYC (their slogan is, "Behind enemy lines since 2005") but it's on its way to the sports bar hall of fame. Every Boston team but the Patriots (OK, a few NYC teams too) have won a championship while diehard Proff Thoms regulars have saturated the walls with a winning spirit. The nachos are huge, Steven Wright watches Sox games sitting at the bar, and they once had a beer named after Bill "The Spaceman" Lee. This bar is Yaz hitting the wall, a last second shot by Bird, a flying leap by Orr. I just wish they served dessert. Believe it or not, it's hard to find a good sports bar in NYC - the kind where a guy is watching a streamed game on his laptop at the bar during March Madness because the 17 games on the TVs are not enough. Now, Proff Thoms also does some interesting counter programming - the upstairs loft hosts "Game of Thrones" nights and was once the place to watch "Lost" where drinkers would get a free beer and sandwich with the "Lost" logo on them. There is even a balcony overlooking second ave for balmy

summer nights. Plus, every July 4th the unofficial official hot dog contest after party is held at Prof Thoms (the contest sponsor does not pick up the tab, but eaters and competitive eating fans do). If you have been amazed at Joey Chestnut's capacity for hot dogs, you should see his record breaking consumption of "Joey Juice" (Double Jack Daniels and Coke with a Jack floater)...drooling is not limited to eating tubesteaks. If you want knowledge-able fans, cute girls, good food, and wise ass managers, plus lobster on Mondays head to Prof Thoms.

1. The Village Idiot (defunct) — The slogan for The Village Idiot was, "the bar you've been practicing for." You wouldn't know it by looking at it... a sloped wooden soaked bar that tilted towards the left center so much that one seat caused beer drippings to fall into one's lap. The walls were falling apart, the bathroom was a mess, and the back room was filled with smoke whether some-one was smoking or not. The owner — a voluminous but kind man named Tom, would drink Guinness until he passed out leaning on the bar, but the stories that fol-lowed the man are legendary. One liquor rep who accom-panied Tom on a junket to the Kentucky Derby said that he bought out the liquor cart and then emptied it almost by himself. When he wanted to hire new bartenders he simply wrote in chalk on the board outside the bar, "Shameless sluts wanted — no experience necessary." In-deed many of the Idiot's beauties would flash the con-struction workers during their "power hour" liquid lunches, often making over $300 in that single hour. Mary Dawn, whom I fell in love with one Winter, would often cover her nipples in duct tape to add to the mystery. The Village Idiot reveled in its low class nature — in the 90s there was a fish tank with snapping turtles and one could purchase three goldfish for a dollar and feed the turtles. I don't think PETA was aware but the regulars who came for Lily or Mary Dawn's brand of humor (and drinking) didn't complain. I loved the place. I loved the

bartenders and occasionally they loved me back — but only for short torrid affairs with no hangovers. As proof that the Village Idiot didn't change (nor its acrid smell) the night the smoking ban in NYC went into effect everyone thought that their clothes wouldn't smell of smoke the next morning — they were wrong — their clothes smelled like Jagermeister. That smell was captured in the coin box of the "Creature from the Black Lagoon" jukebox that my buddy Levi acquired from Tom, when the bar was closing. Levi would let people smell the inside of the machine and they always identified it as the Idiot's signature odor. Plus, the fruit flies in it wouldn't die, but Levi sold the machine for his highest price ever — the buyer had never seen art work so pristine as if the machine was brand new. Levi mentioned, quite truthfully, that sunlight had not hit the art in twenty years — the back room had no windows and the despite creatures from the beer lagoon puking by (and once inside) the machine — the pinball art was perfect. So was the bar. Tom would own a bar, but set the low prices and when the neighborhood gentrified he would move on. Today, you can see the beginnings of the next Idiot at places like Spanky and Darla's, The Duck, and most notably, The Patriot which has some of the Village's flair, but needs time soaked booze to pickle the place to perfection. One can find old photos of past Village Idiot bartenders but online is only one of the beautiful temptress Mary Dawn — ripped tank tee shirt, cowboy hat, and Jack Daniels raised like the Stanley Cup. It is a moment in time, for a bar long gone, that I had the pleasure of witnessing. Belly to the bar, drinkers craved that history in a bottle and the Village Idiot opened its doors and its heart for our livers and lives.

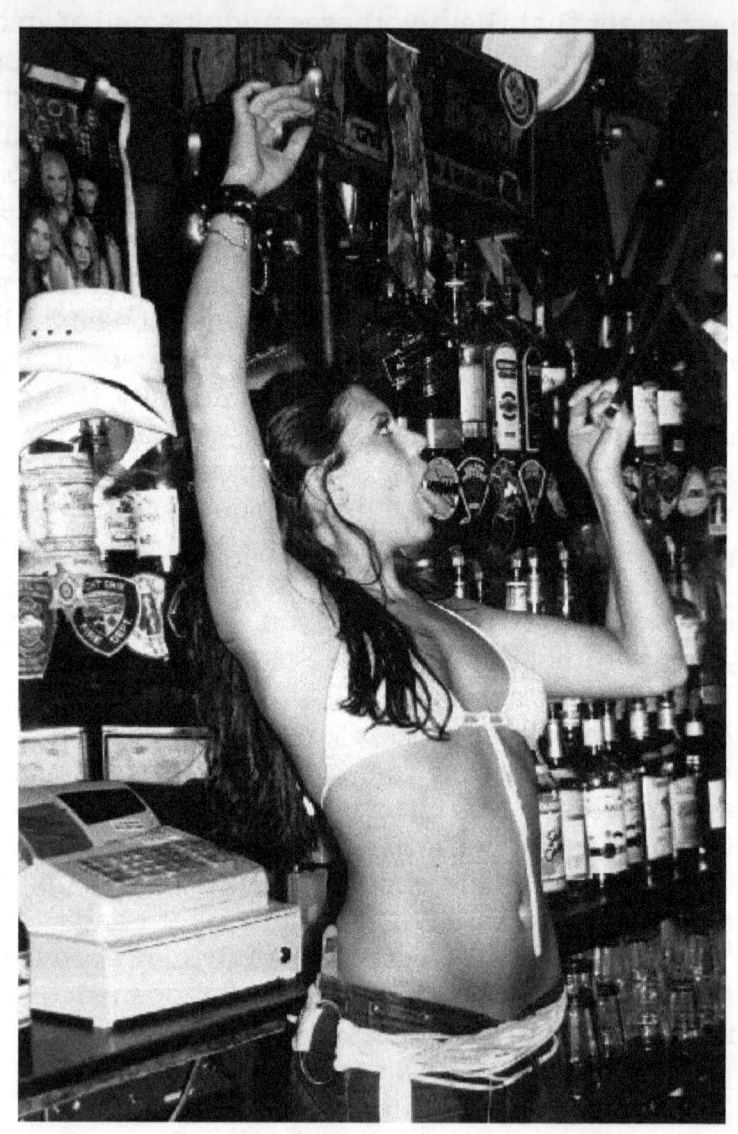

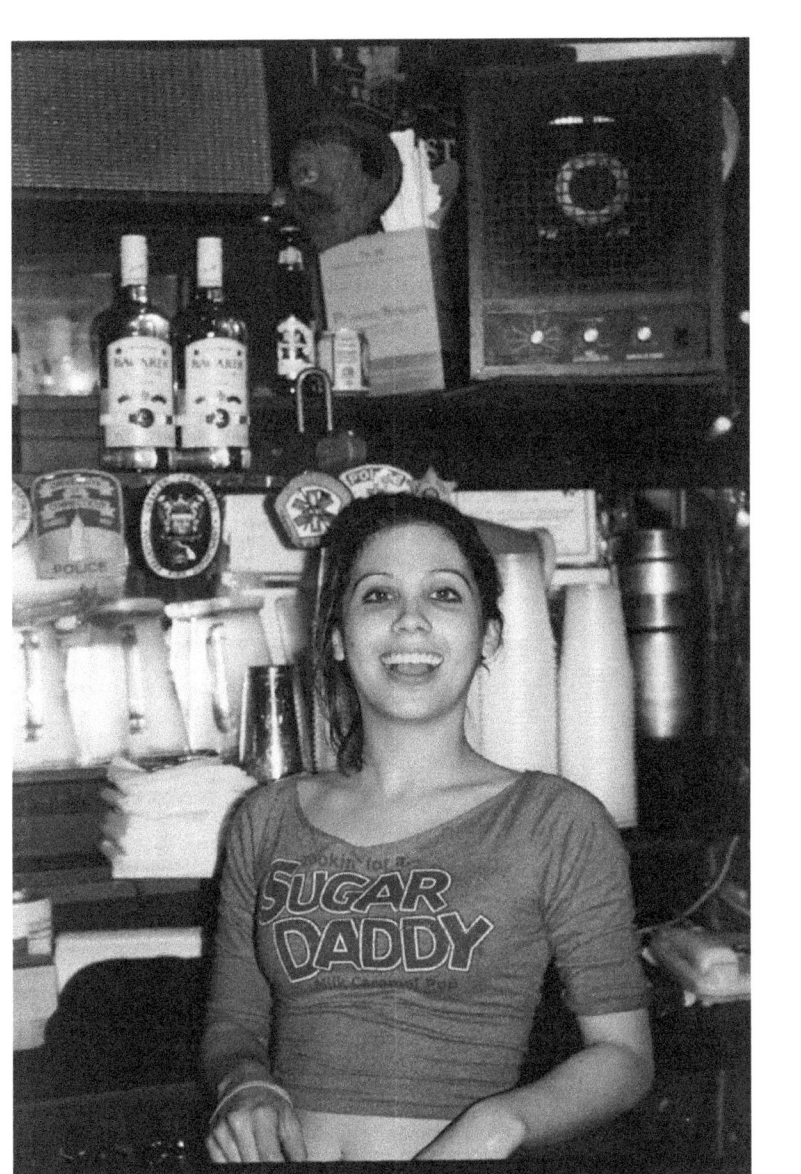

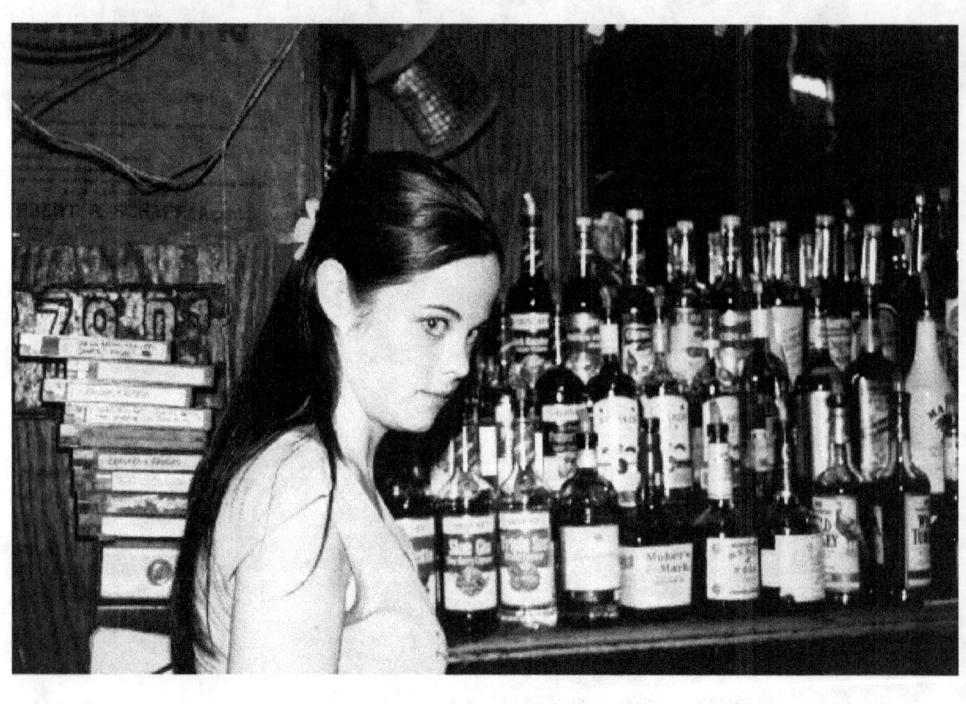

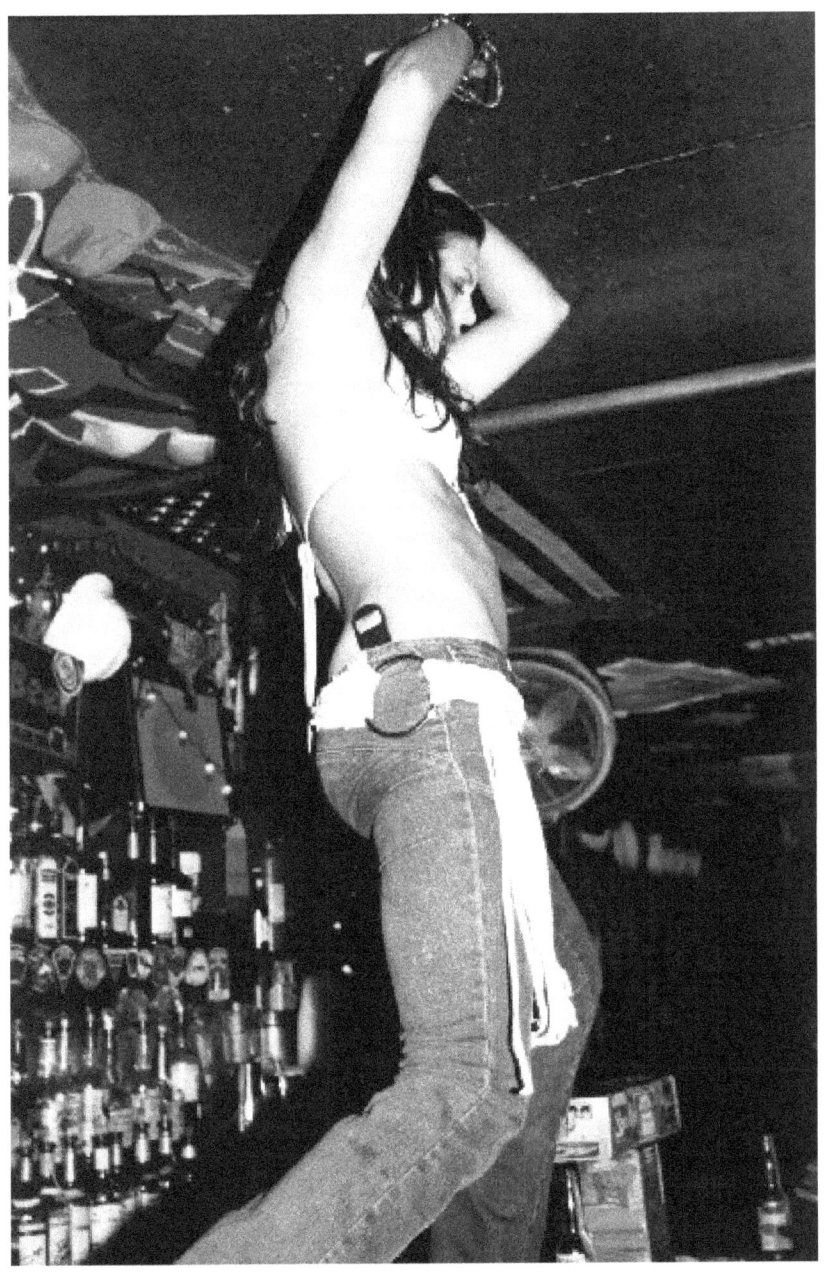

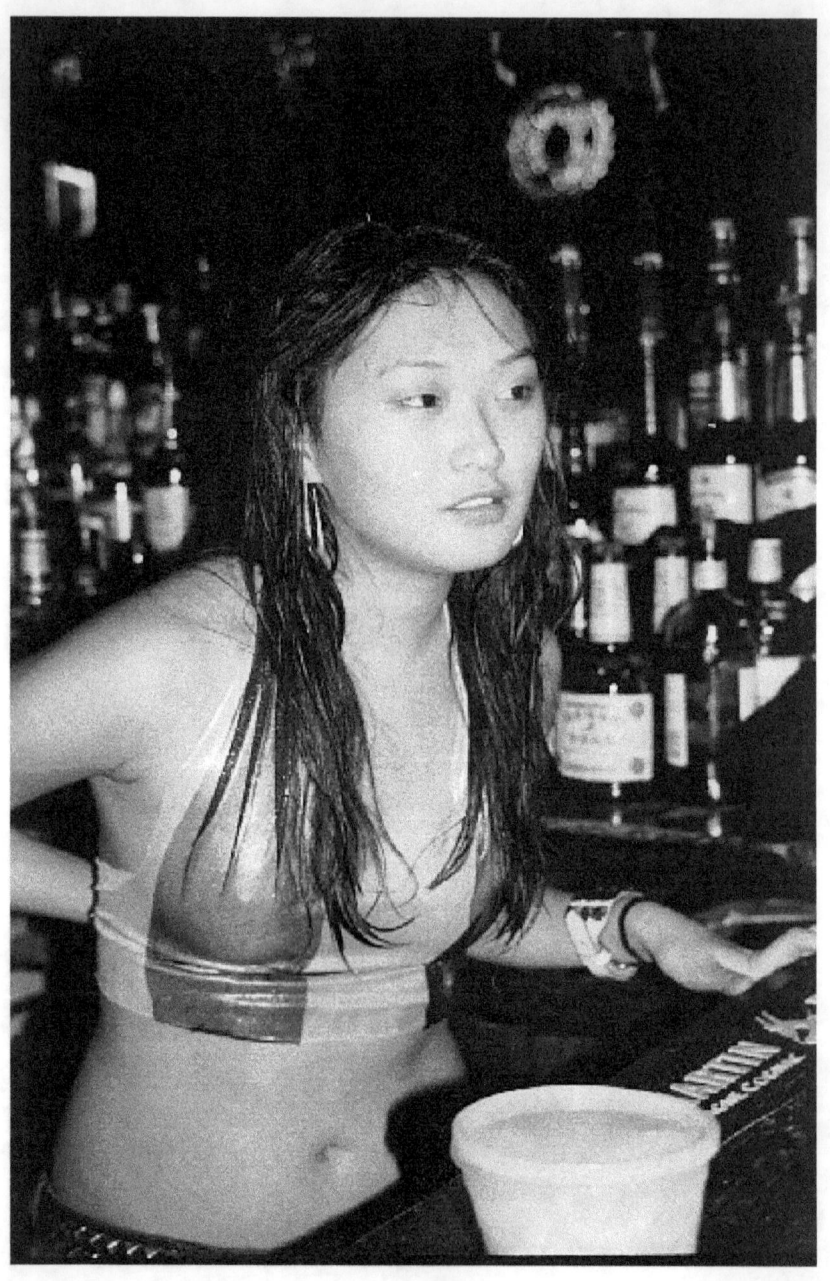

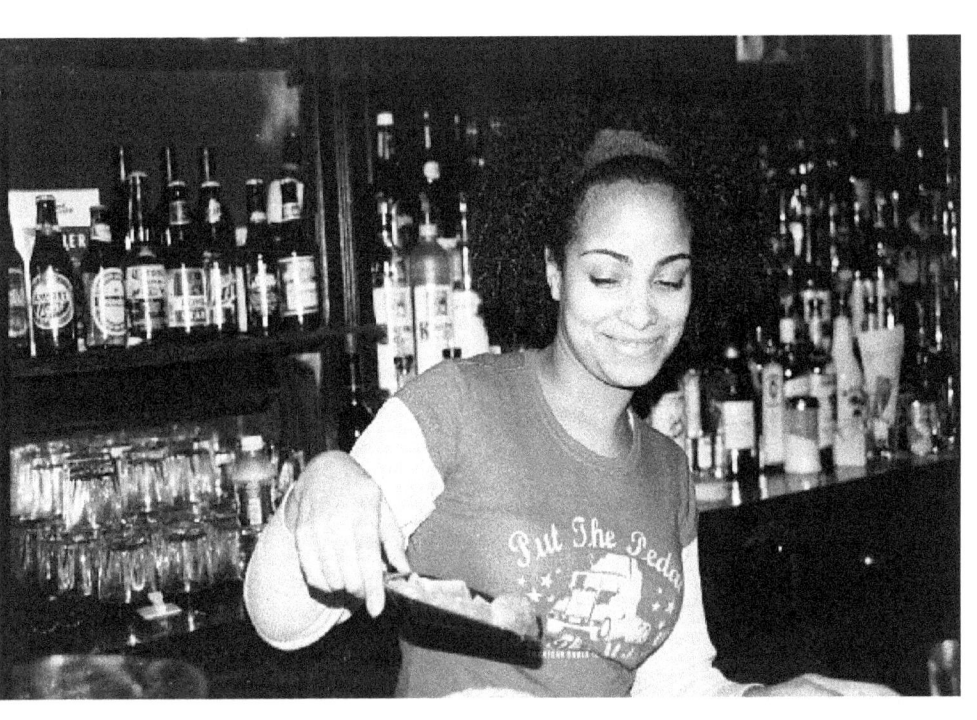

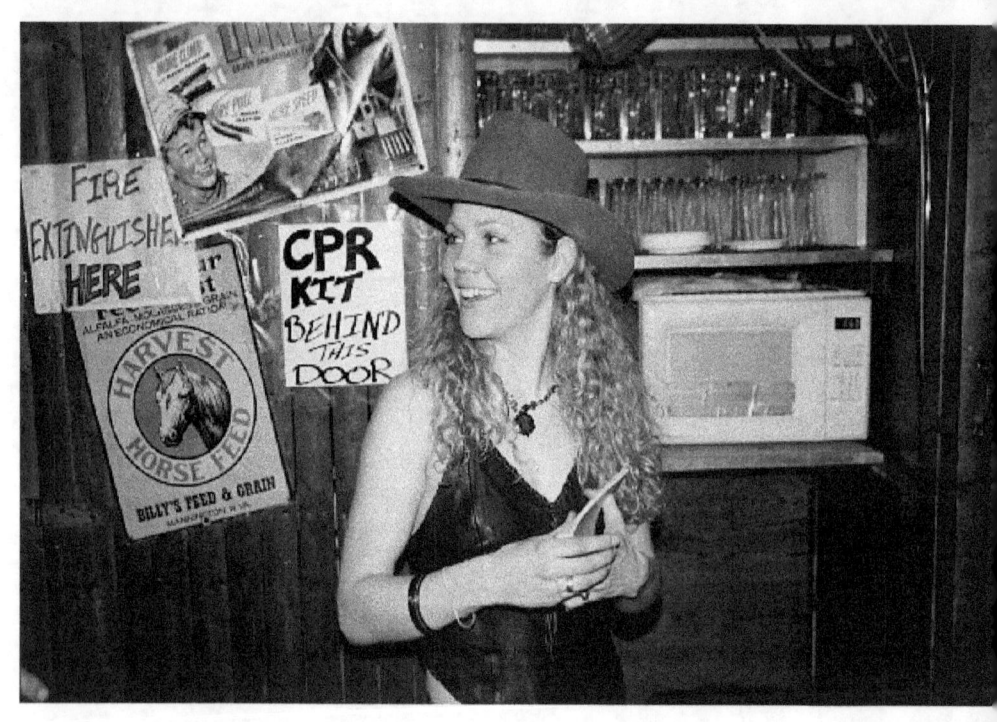

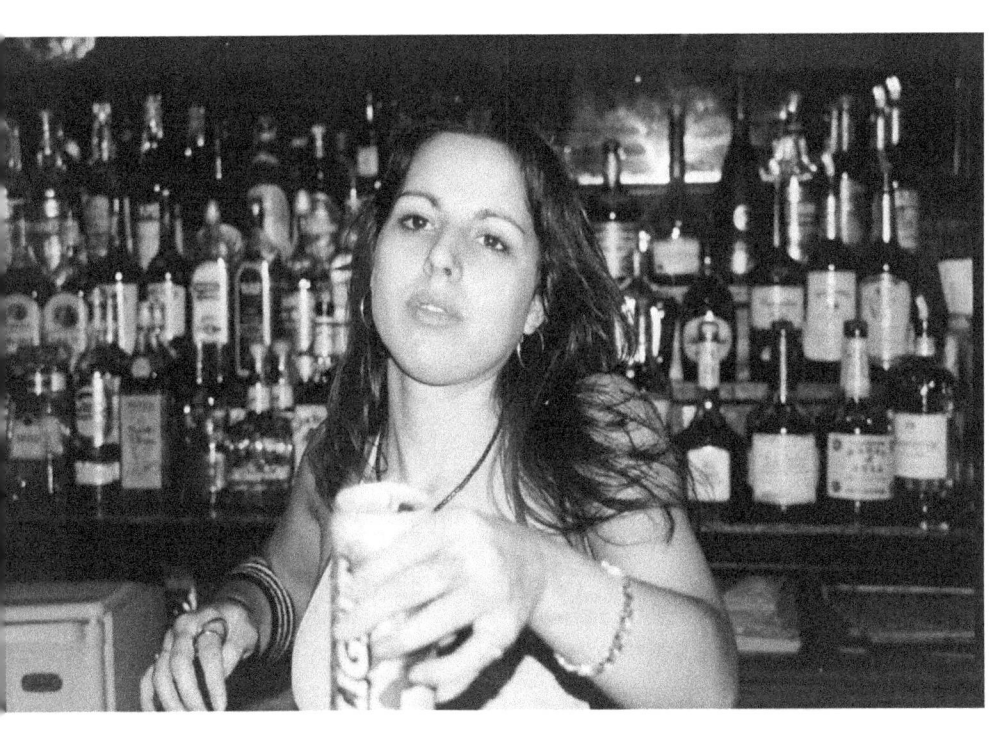

Dive Bar Beauty — Anna at Coyote Ugly

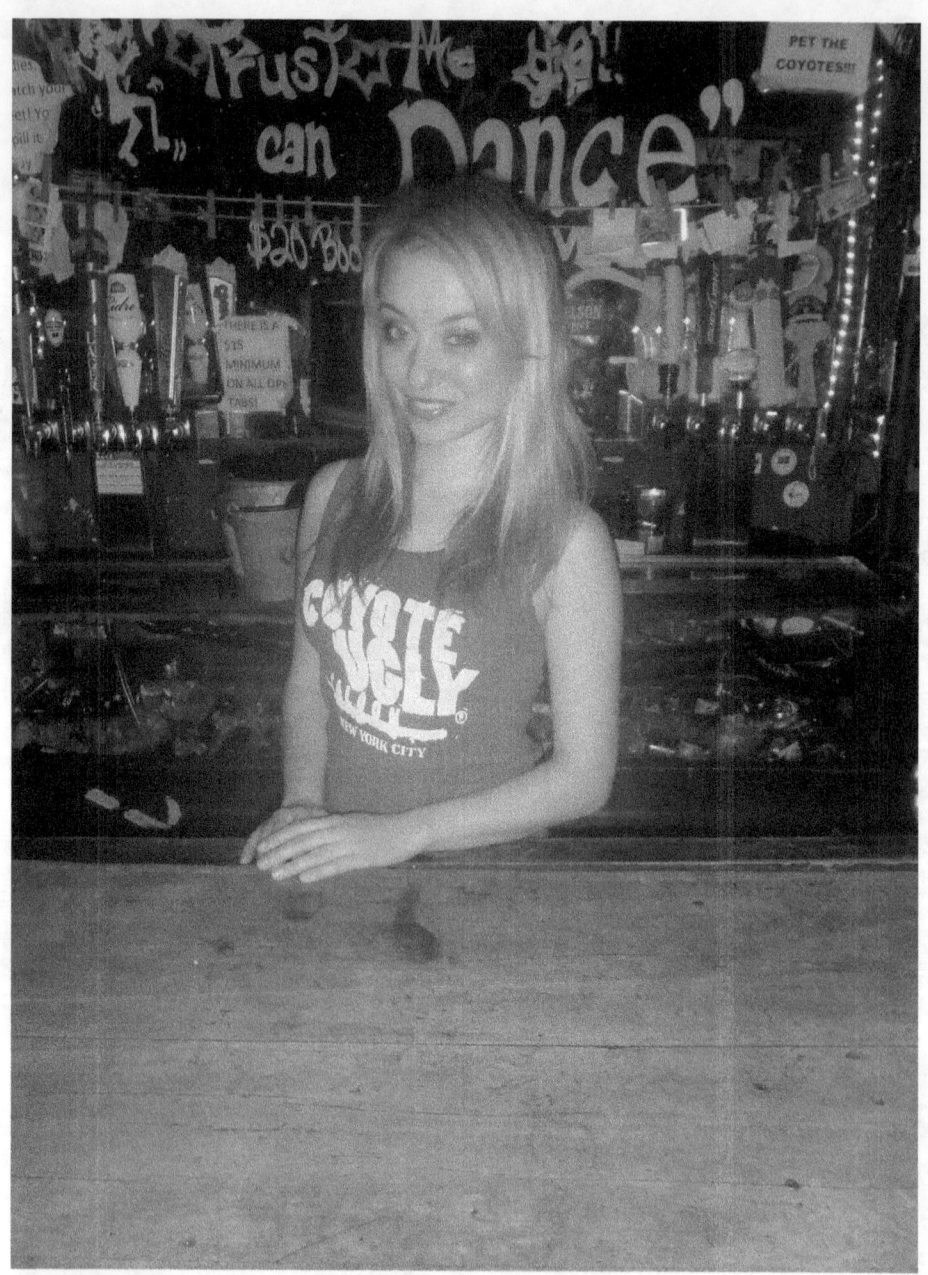

02/26/2014

The shiny shimmy of a naked thigh, the thrust of a curvaceous hip, the high kick and twist... this is not Olympic ice dancing, nor a stripper working the pole... the flash of cured blond hair and lipstick smile appear, as does the bottle of rotgut tequila that is poured down your throat as you gag, fall in love, and try to cheer louder as the stunning Anna atop the Coyote Ugly bar yells, "Let's hear it for Wednesday." And the roar of the crowd over the cranked juke box tells you that this is where to be on a rainy Wednesday afternoon and no where else. The upcoming Sports Illustrated Swimsuit issue has nothing on Anna, who is clad in tight (very tight) jean shorts and a purple bra. When Anna is working, I play Katy Perry's sexually suggestive, "Peacock," and with it's chorus, comes Anna's signature dance move — he pretends to have a giant imaginary penis and with a scowl, she slaps it with both hands. The censors on "So You Think You Can Dance" would never let this phallic flogging pass, but if you don't think a hot chick air slapping an invisible penis is hot... you just don't know Anna. So, in the interests of journalist professionalism and limiting my number of Bushmill's Black Bush shots... let's get to know Anna.

You are from the Ukraine, but how long have you lived in NYC and why did you move?

I have lived in New York City for six years. I moved because I had difficulty with my country — I had a linguistics degree but couldn't get a normal job. I wanted to travel and see the world. I could have gone to Germany or the US. I want to stay in the US and become a nurse and have a steady paycheck.

Do you use your Linguistics degree at Coyote Ugly?

No... I use dirty words instead.

How long have you been a Coyote and why here?

I have been at Coyote Ugly for 1 year and three months. I didn't understand the concept of the dive bar bartender mentality — I was too shy. You need an American mentality.

How hard was the audition process?

For me, I did not audition. The manager here saw my photo on Facebook from another bar and offered me the job. There was no audition because at the time, Coyote Ugly had an urgent need for bartenders. After three days here, shyness goes away. Partying seems fun while auditioning but it's hard to pretend to be someone else — not all girls can do it.

Is there a lot of competition between the bartenders?

Maybe jealousy. We are encouraged to sell merchandise and shots and we are told who is the best. When I started it was harder like when you work with all females but the current team is good.

What is a typical day or night like hour wise? Energy wise? How often are you dancing on the bar?

I commute from Coney Island so it's an hour and half during the day and an hour and forty minutes at night. It is around a fourteen hour day, but it's not physically exhausting... it's mentally exhausting. I am dancing every other song at night because there are three bartenders, but during the day it is more interaction.

Where did you come up with the slapping the invisible penis move?

A very disturbing childhood (Laughs) I would watch American rappers with weird moves that are corny. That is where the move is from.

What are the regulars like? What are the females who come in here like?

All the regulars are men — some I've known for two years from my previous bartending job. Sometimes I forget that I am working hard, it seems like hanging out with friends. Tourists come in and want to have as much fun as possible in short time. Regulars get more personal. I like to find conversation with people I care. Women come to the bar to feel sexy. Desirable and pretty. Dancing on the bar she can feel a certain way. I feel pretty good about myself when I am up there.

What do you drink while you are working?

I drink the same when I go out — vodka or tequila. I like Patron Tequila.

How would you describe your fashion style?

Regular - although I was not confident about my body before I worked here. I never bought a separate bikini, but after working at Coyote Ugly, I bought one for the beach but I also wear it to work

What is the first thing you do when you get home?

Eat and sleep — I eat mostly Ukrainian and Russian food.

How do you stay in such great shape?

Working here it is easy — you don't eat and you dance a lot. It is like a gym every day at work.

One serious question — how is the situation in the Ukraine, especially Kiev affecting you?

It is hard to judge the people of Ukraine. I have never gone back, but you can't be violent even if you are fighting for something. I feel badly for the policemen who are doing their job while their mothers worry.

Who is your favorite Coyote and why?

I have two favorites — Maya has been here two years and she is so confident she can just turn on a crowd. She has a stunning body and I love her personality. No matter how sick she always manages her mood. Kay is the most crazy person and she does whatever she wants to. I want to become like her. I like her.

Will you be working the 21st year anniversary?

It is Sunday, March 23rd and I will be working.

Why no boyfriend?

A bartender should always be single, but never available.

Would you ever date a customer?
No.

Where do you take your fan mail or social media? When can the fans come see you in person?

The funny thing is that I am not that social. When I go out it is to the library or a café shop. I am on the Coyote Ugly Facebook page and I work daytime Weds, Friday, and Saturday. Come see me... and buy some shots!

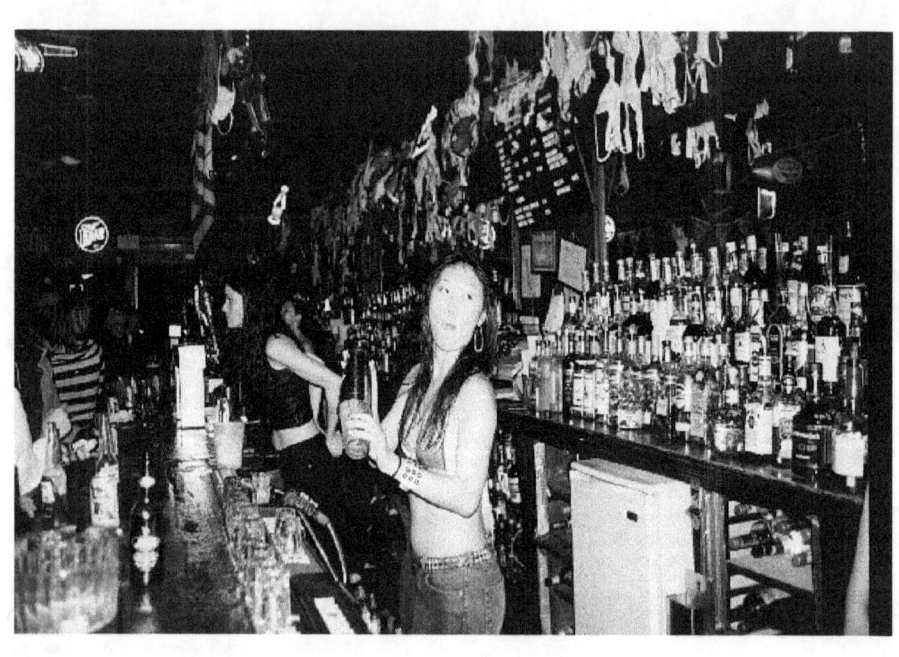

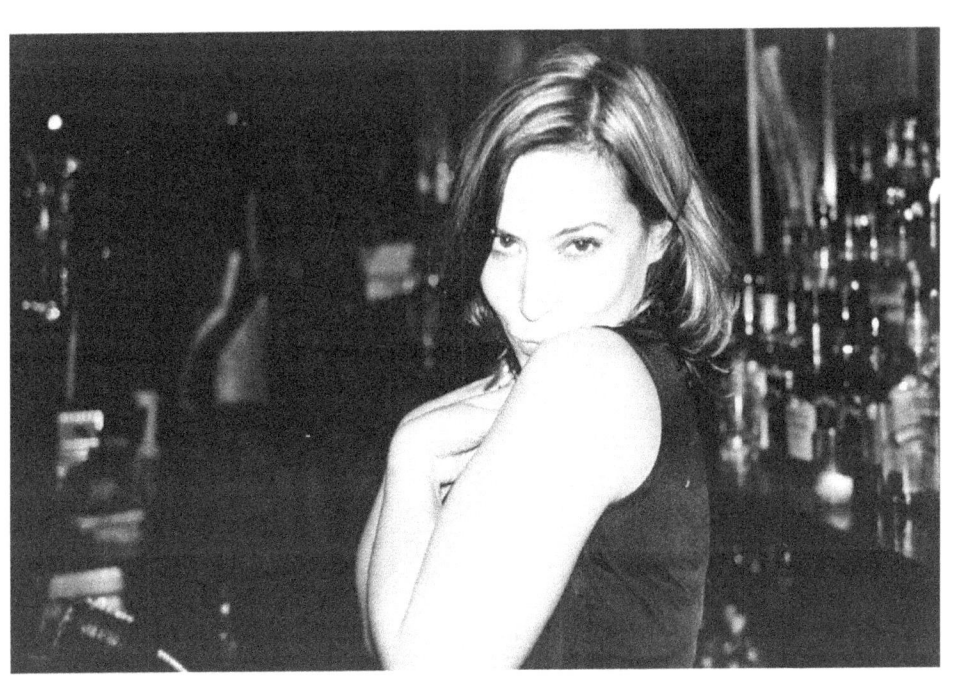

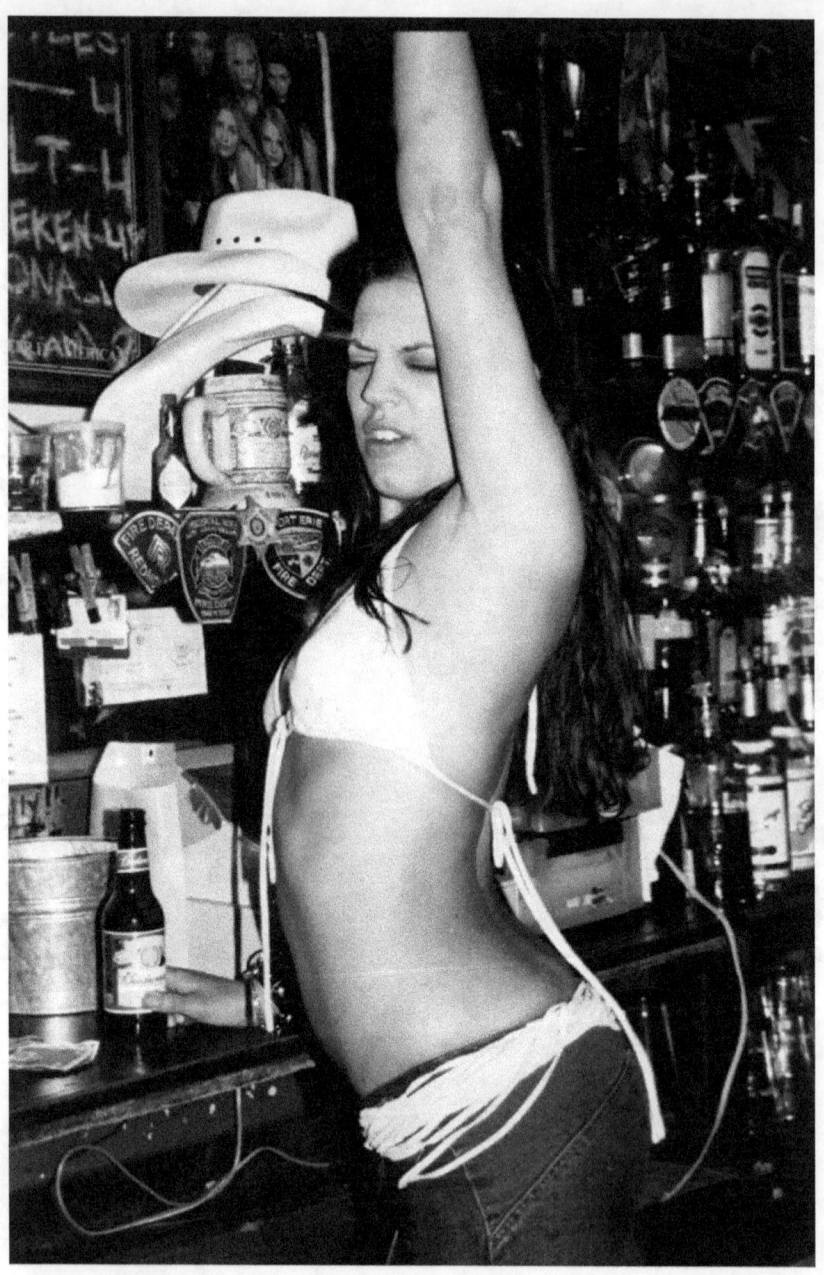

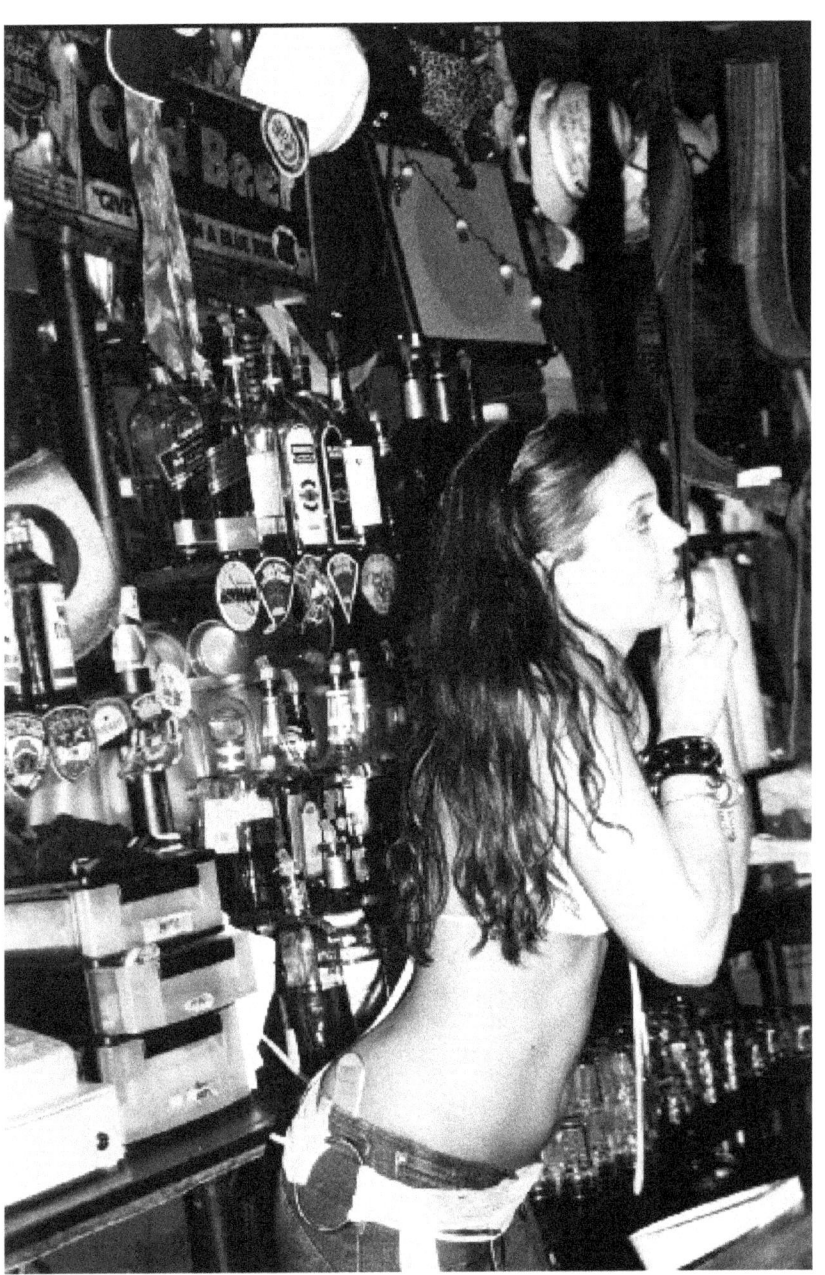

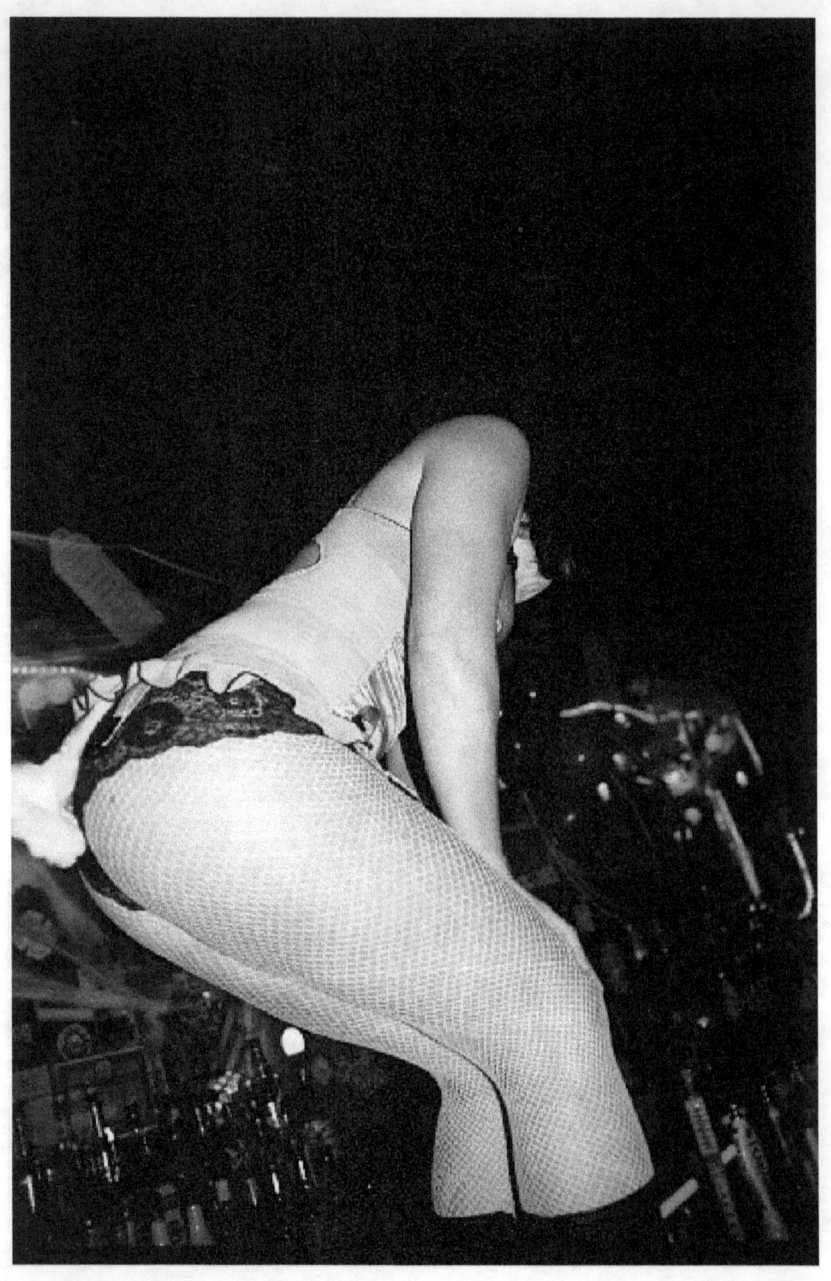

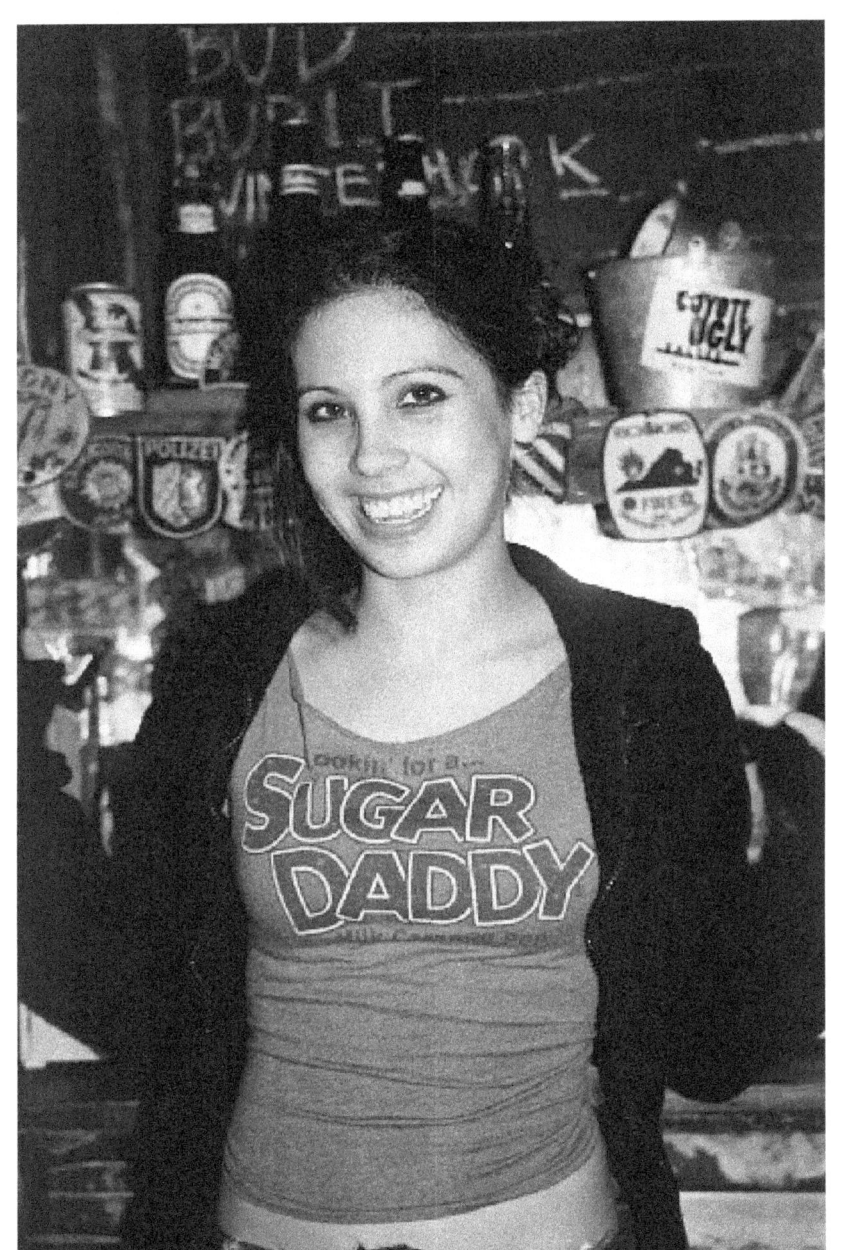

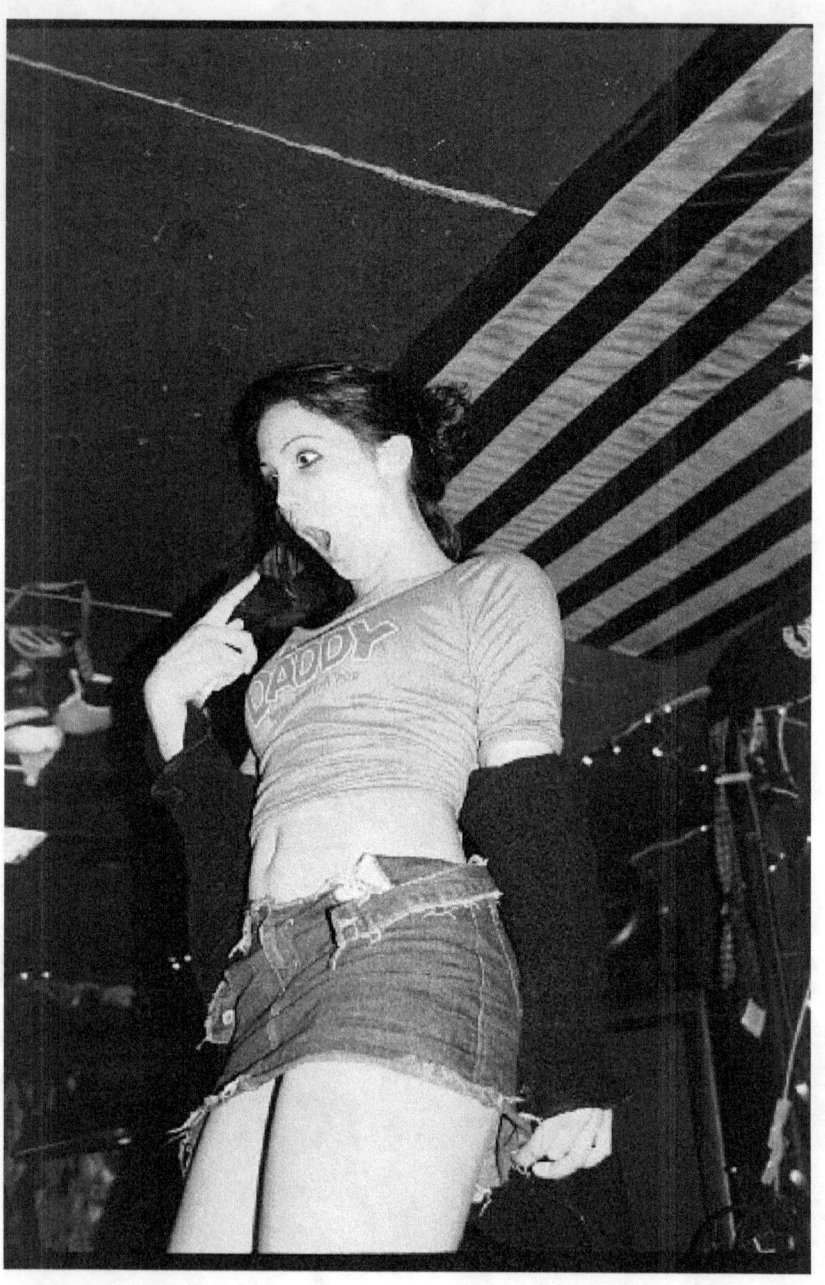

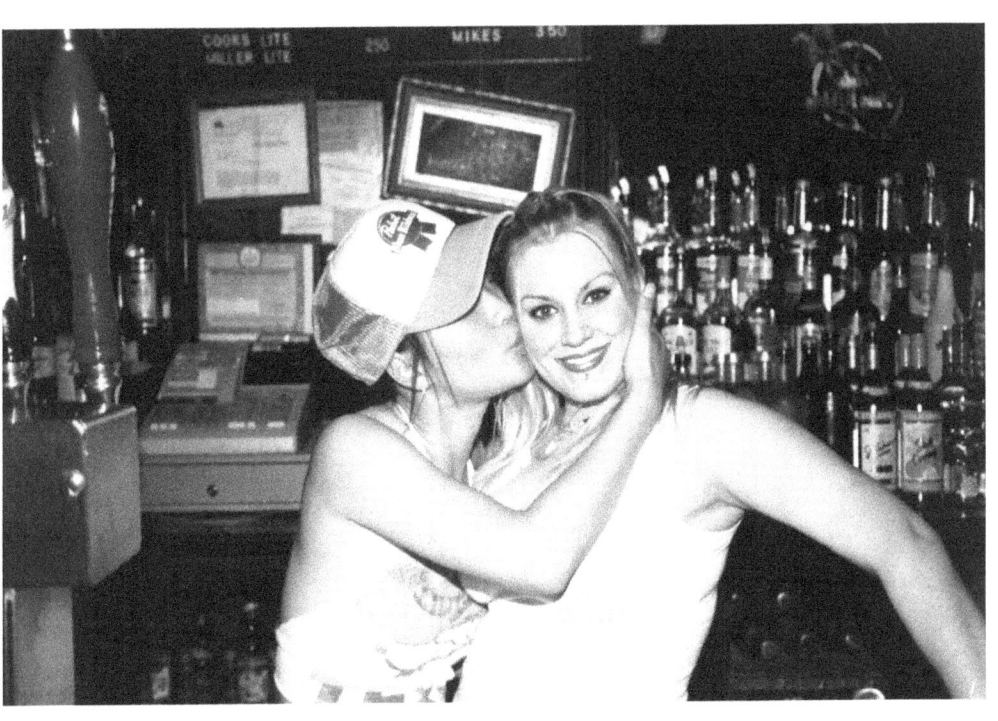

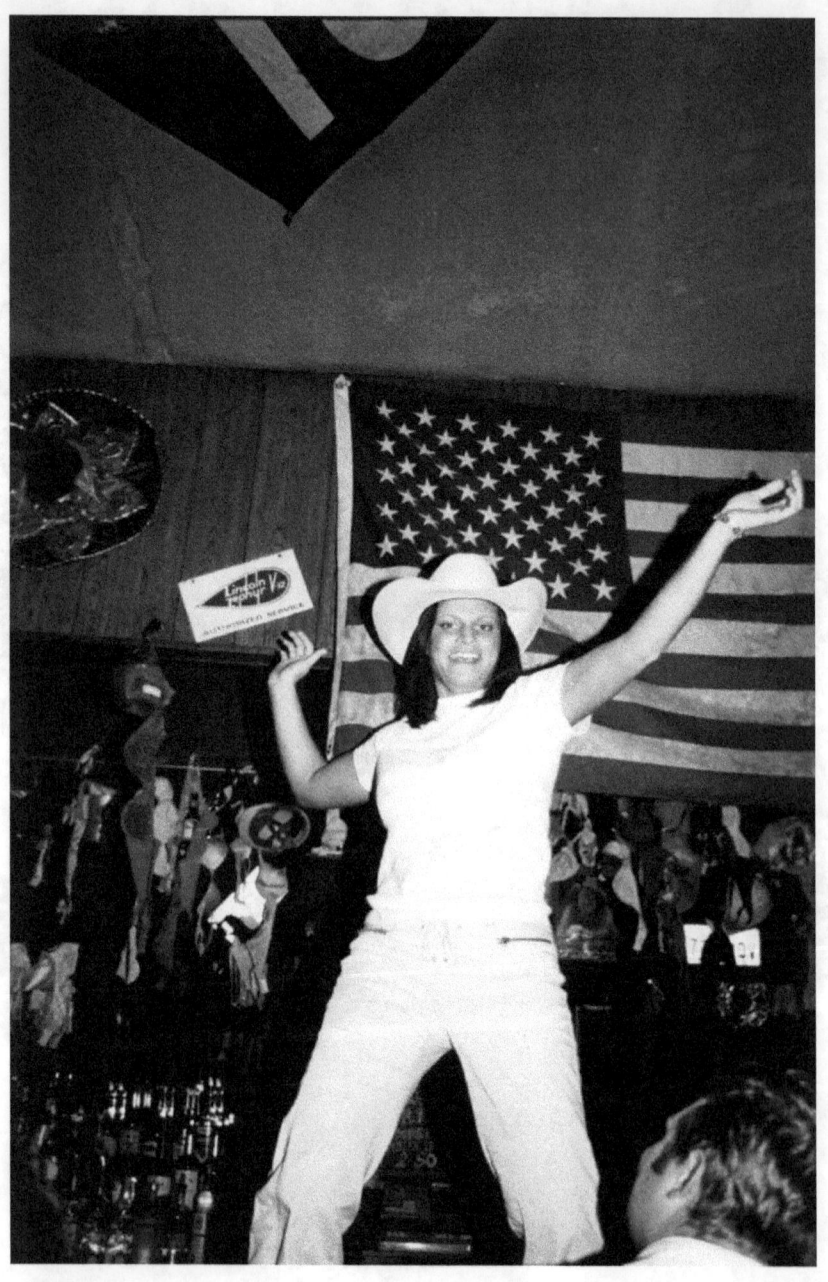

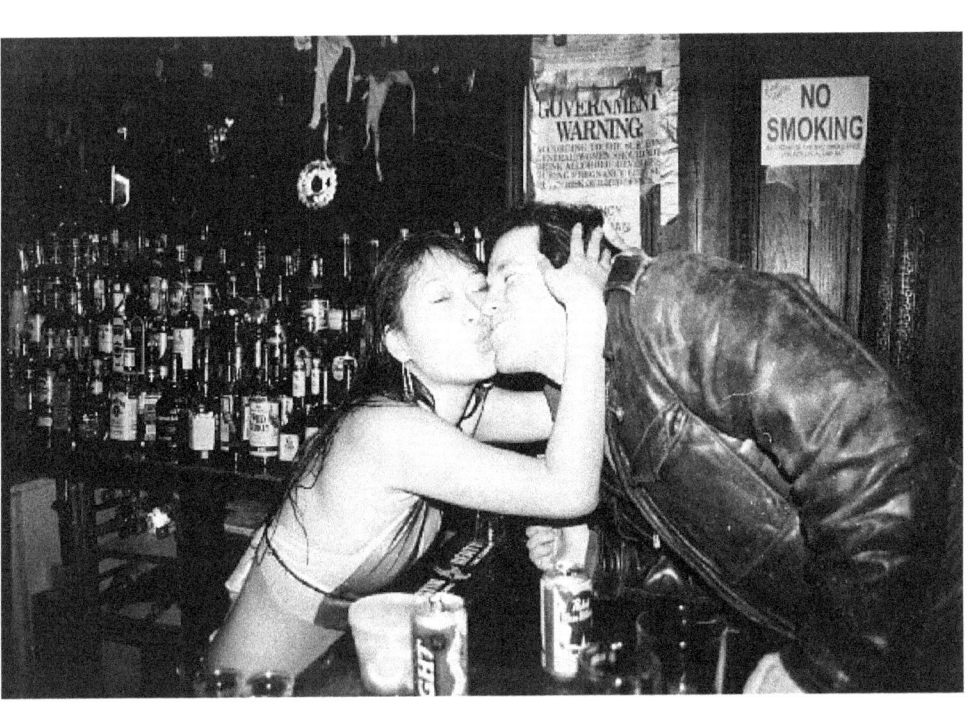

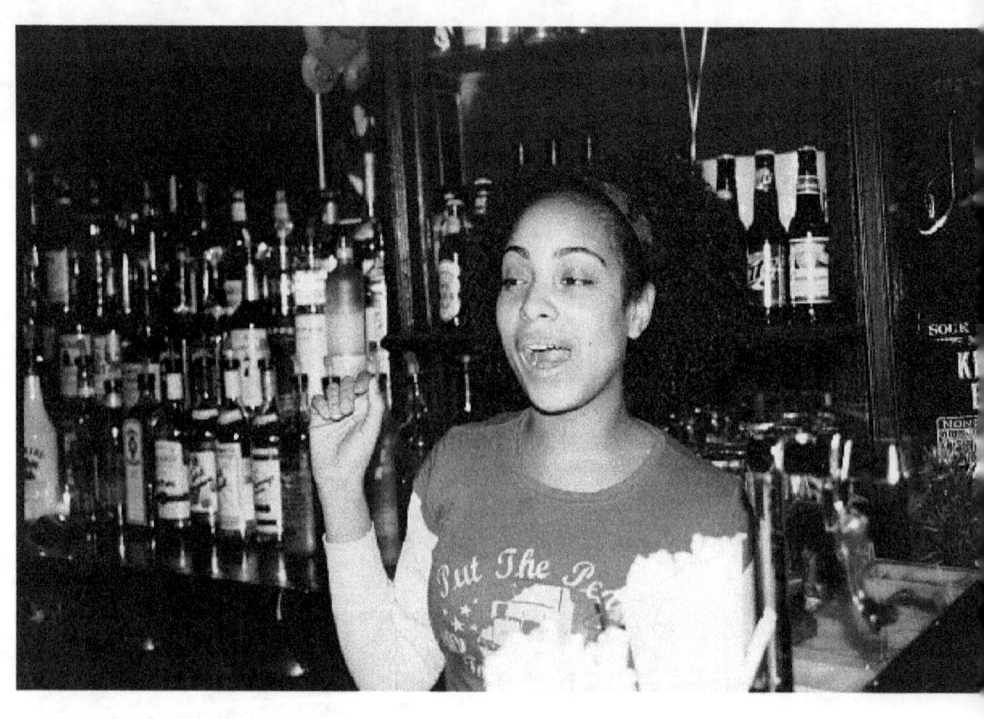

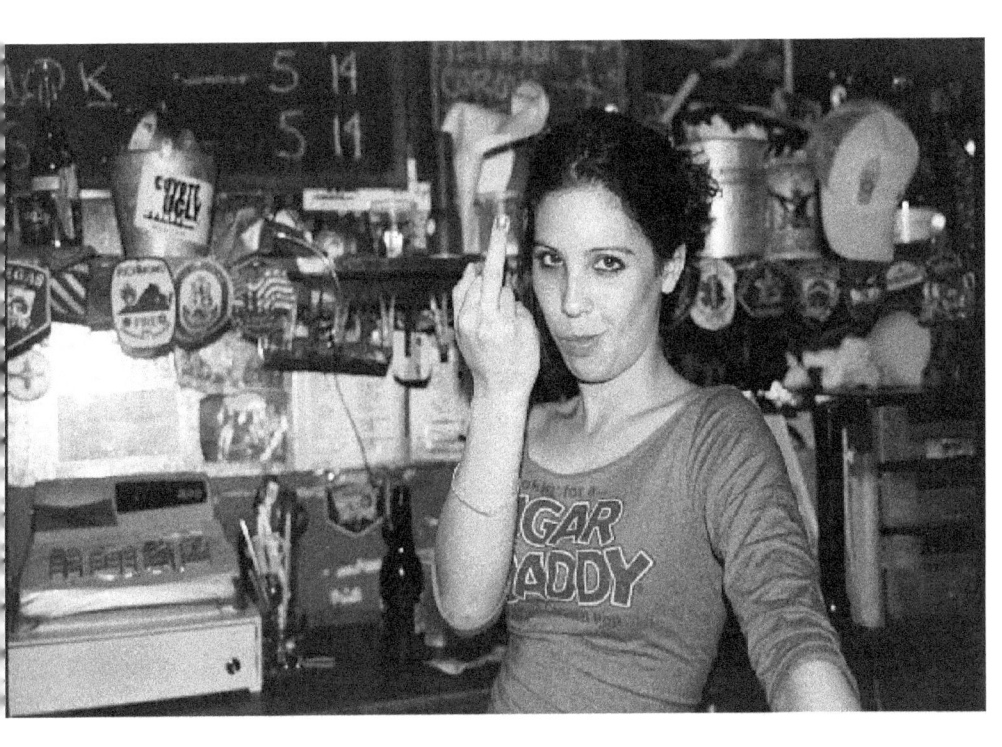

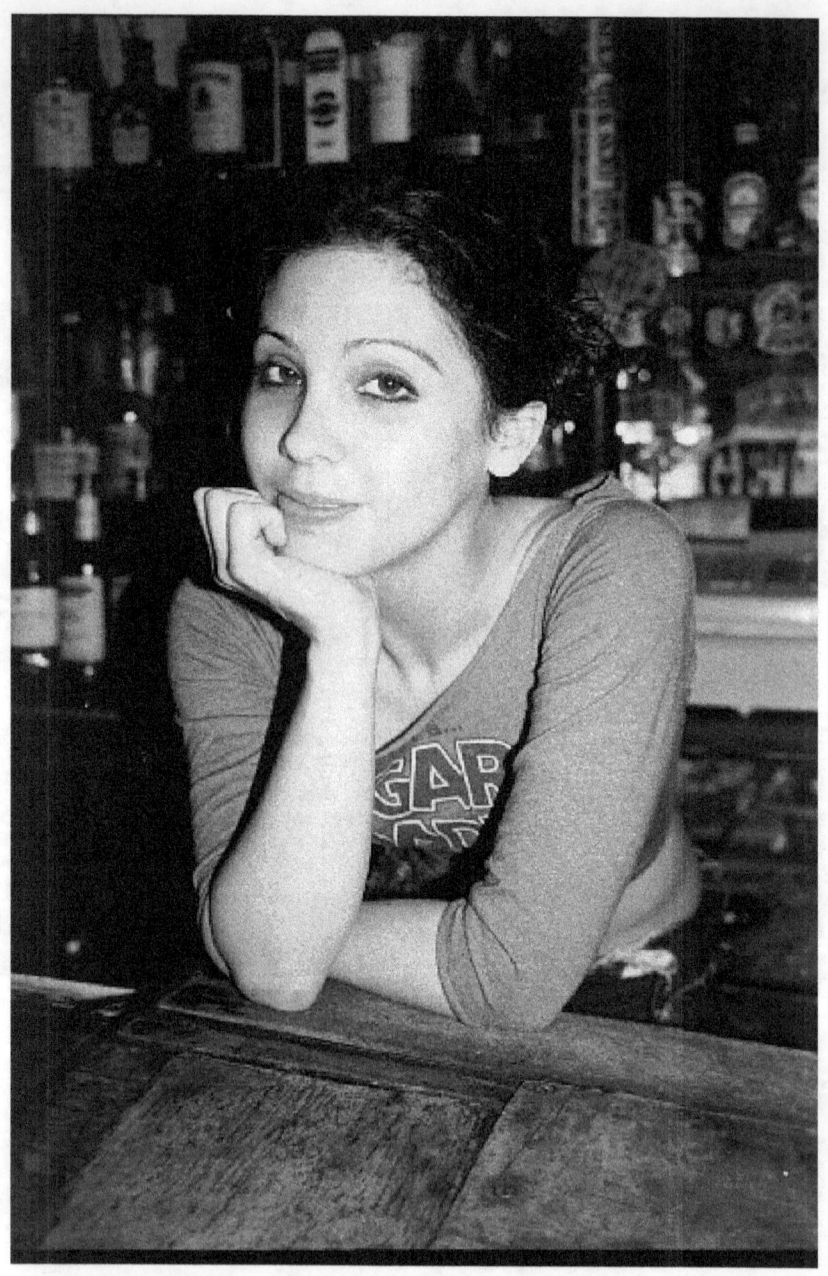

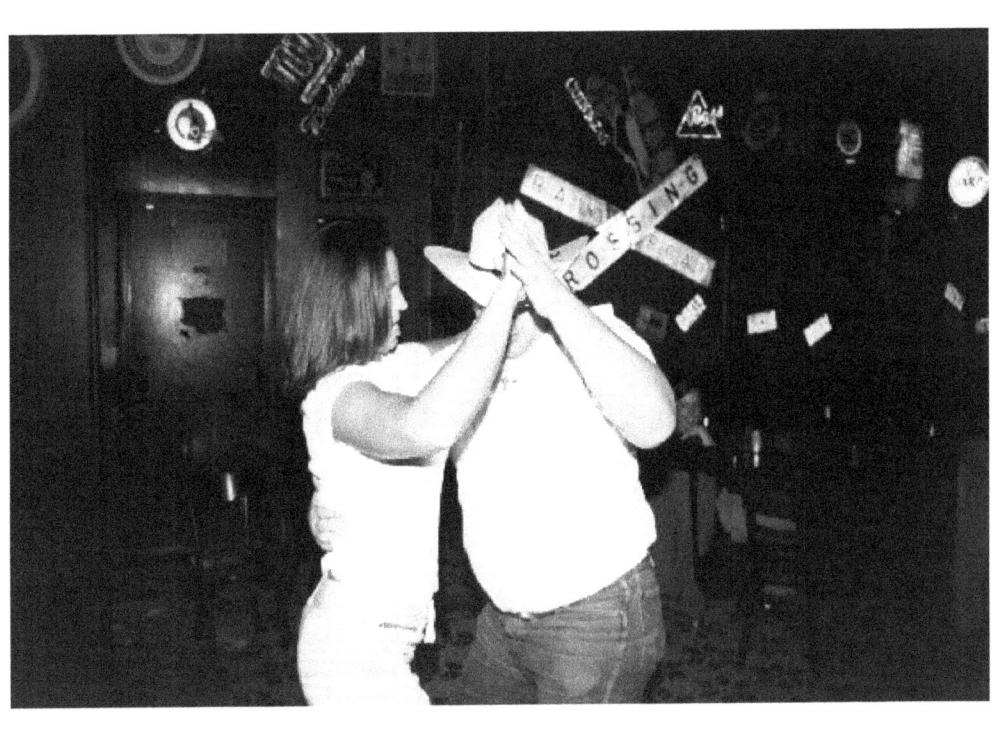

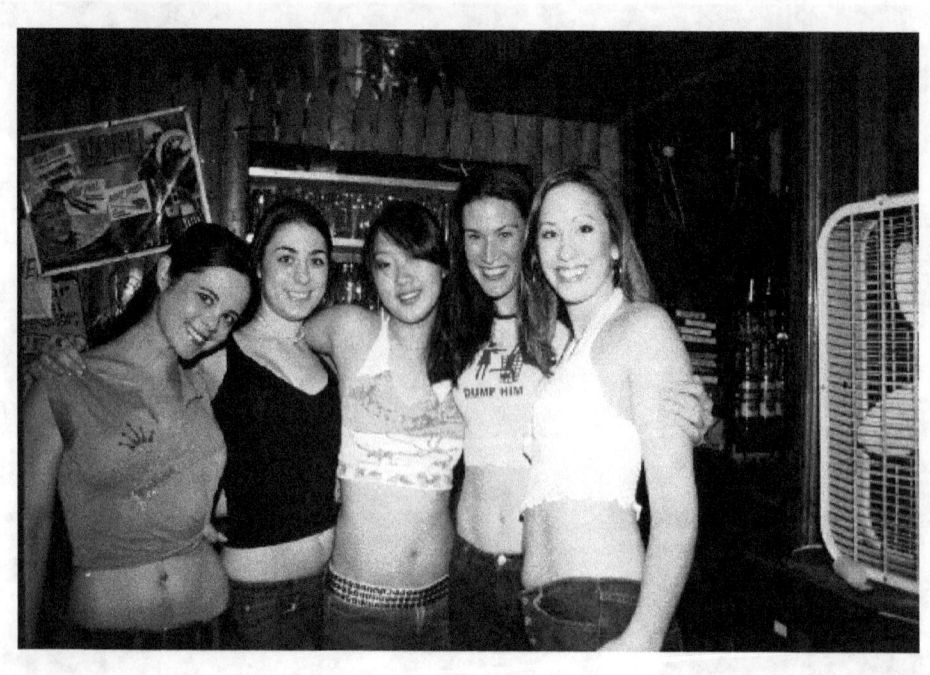

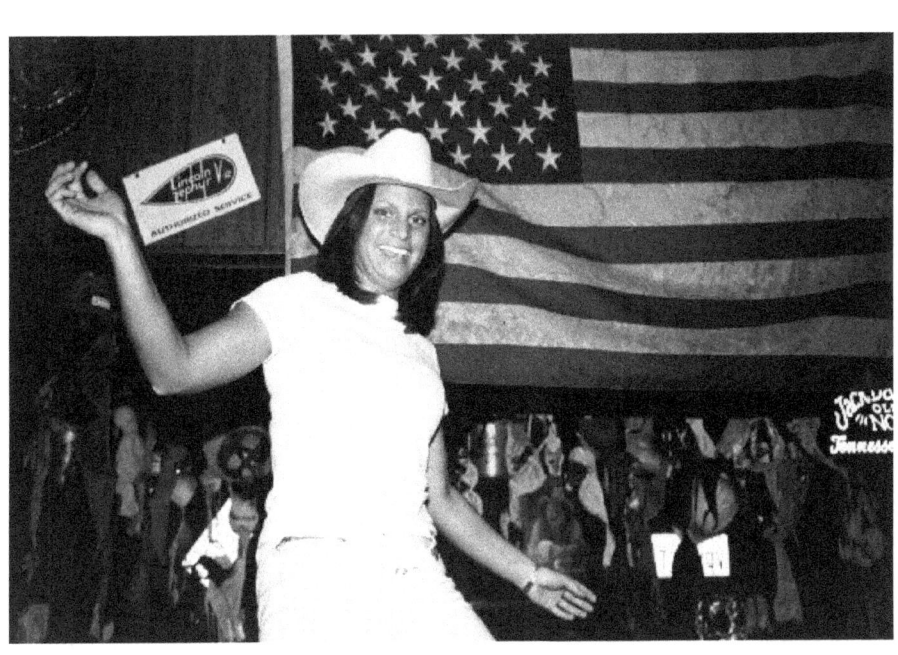

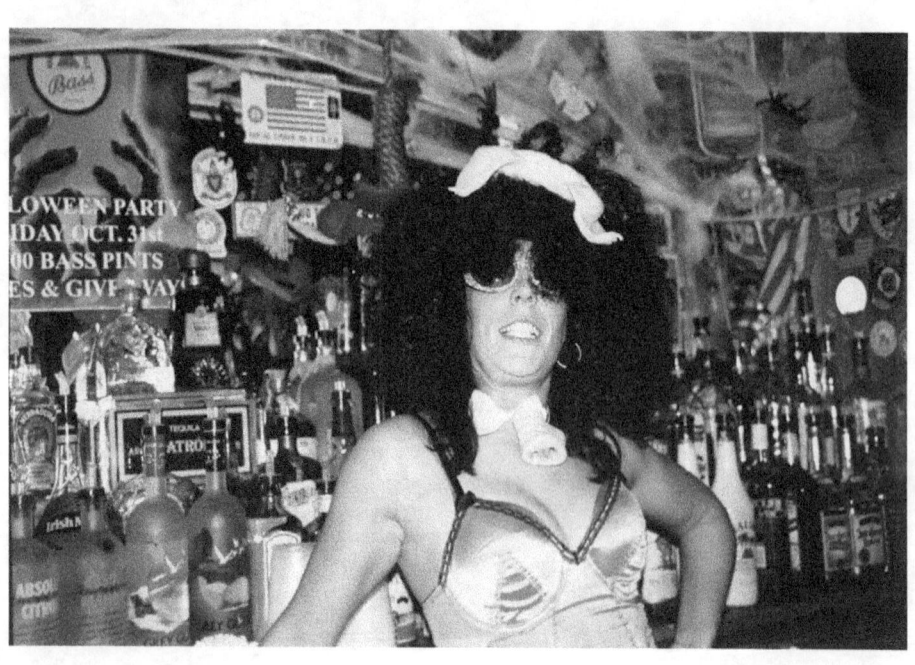

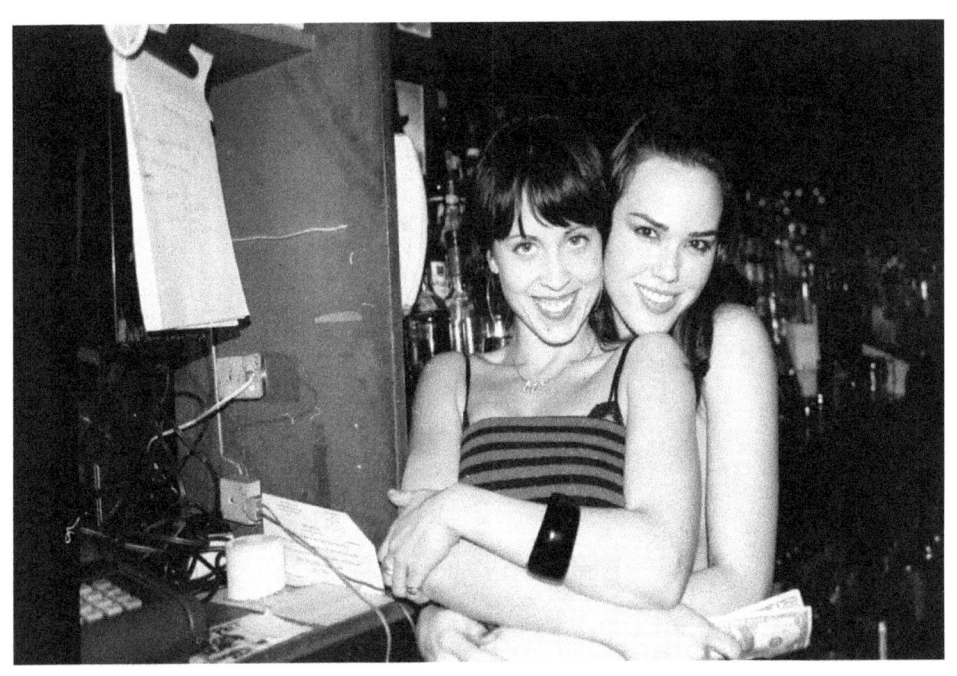

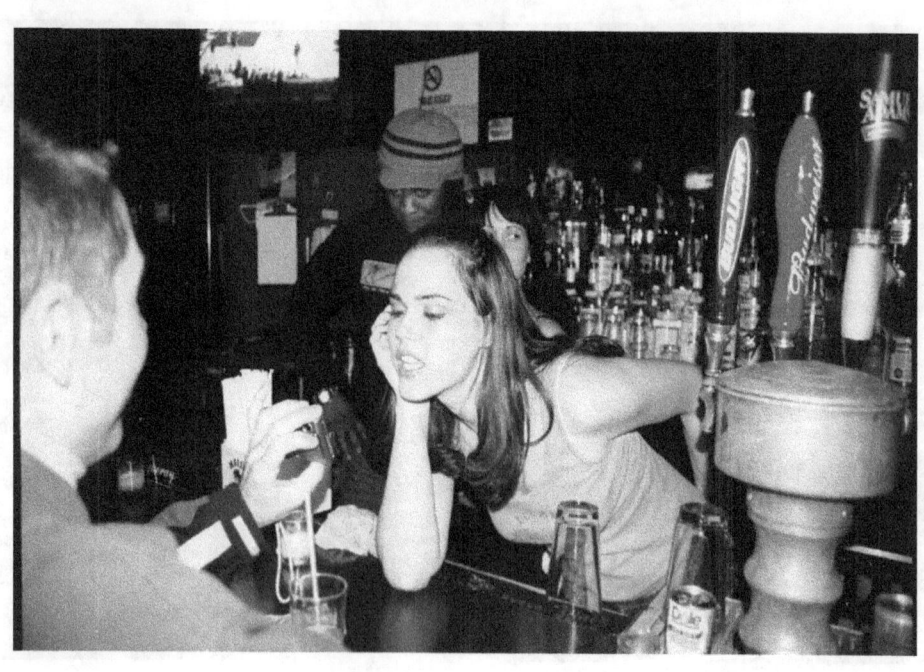

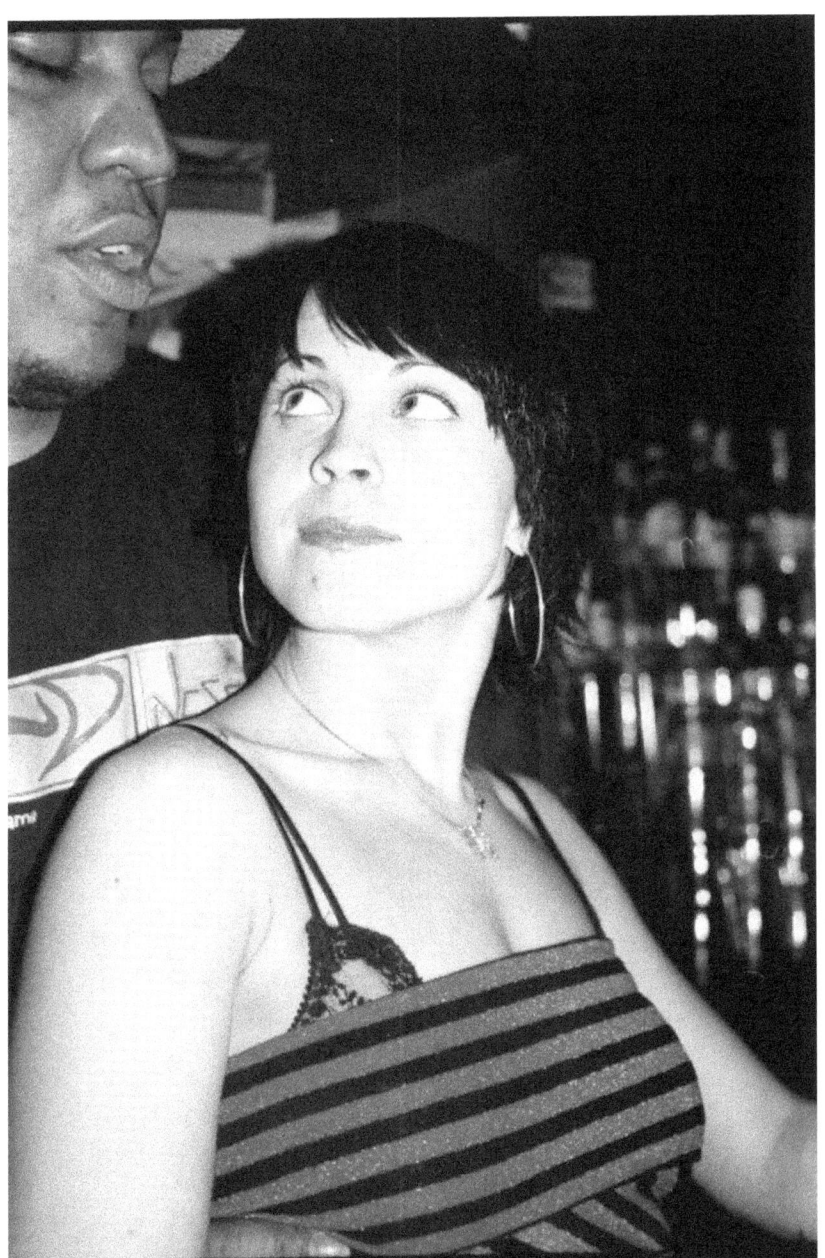

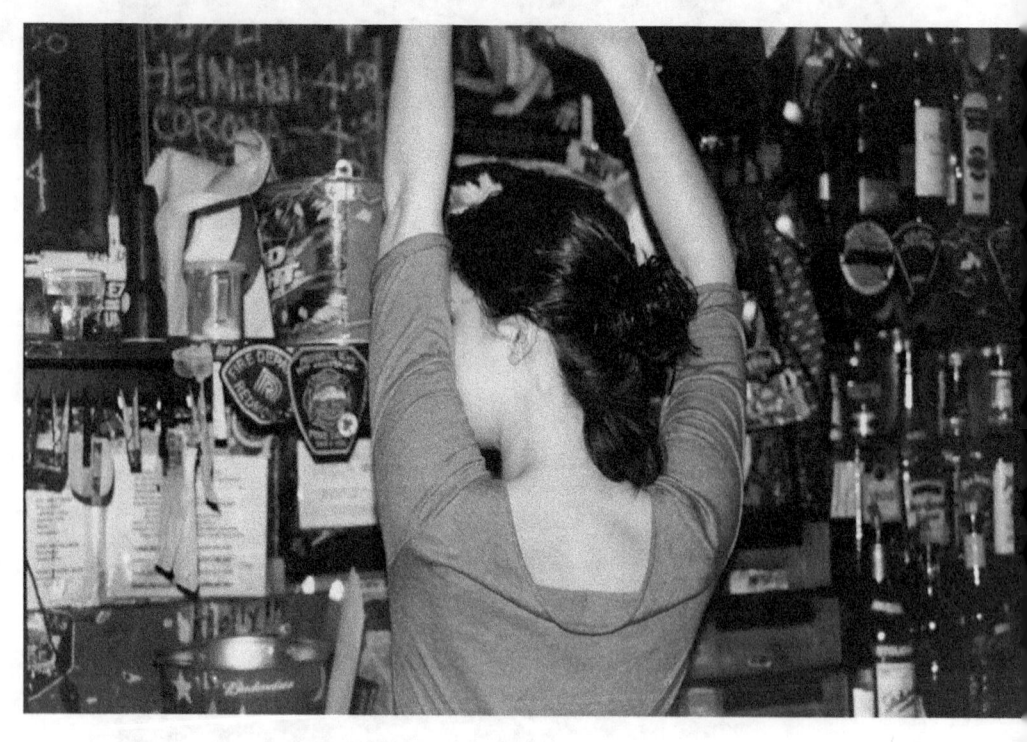

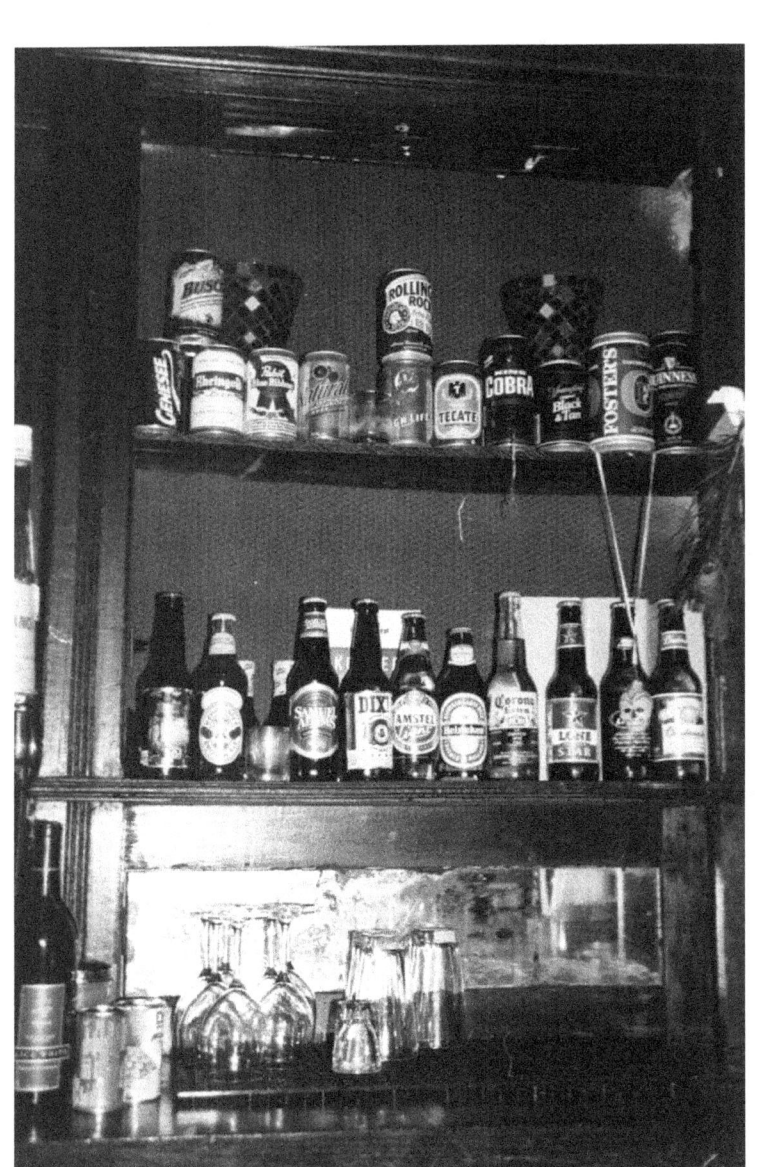

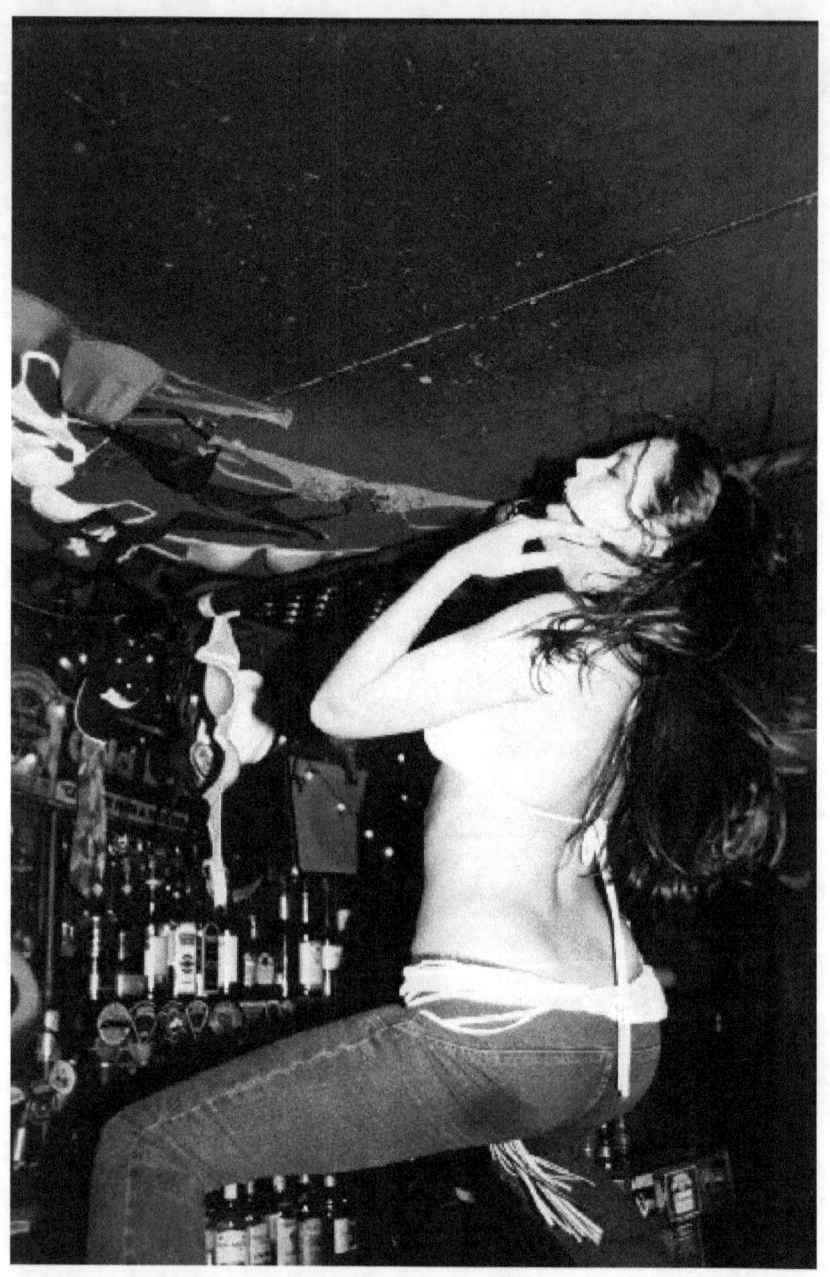

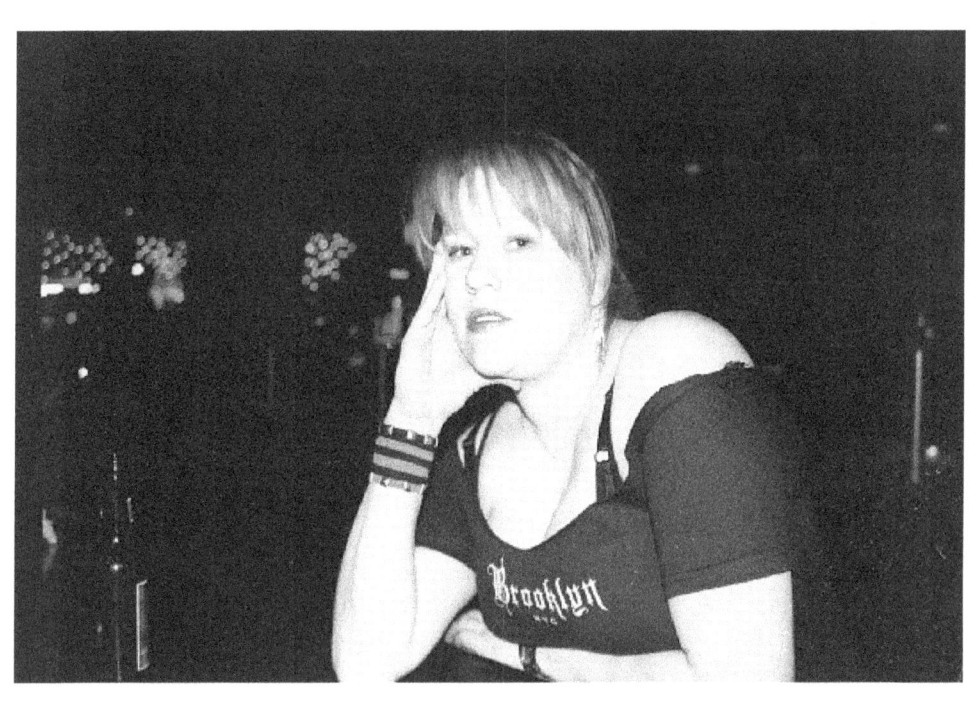

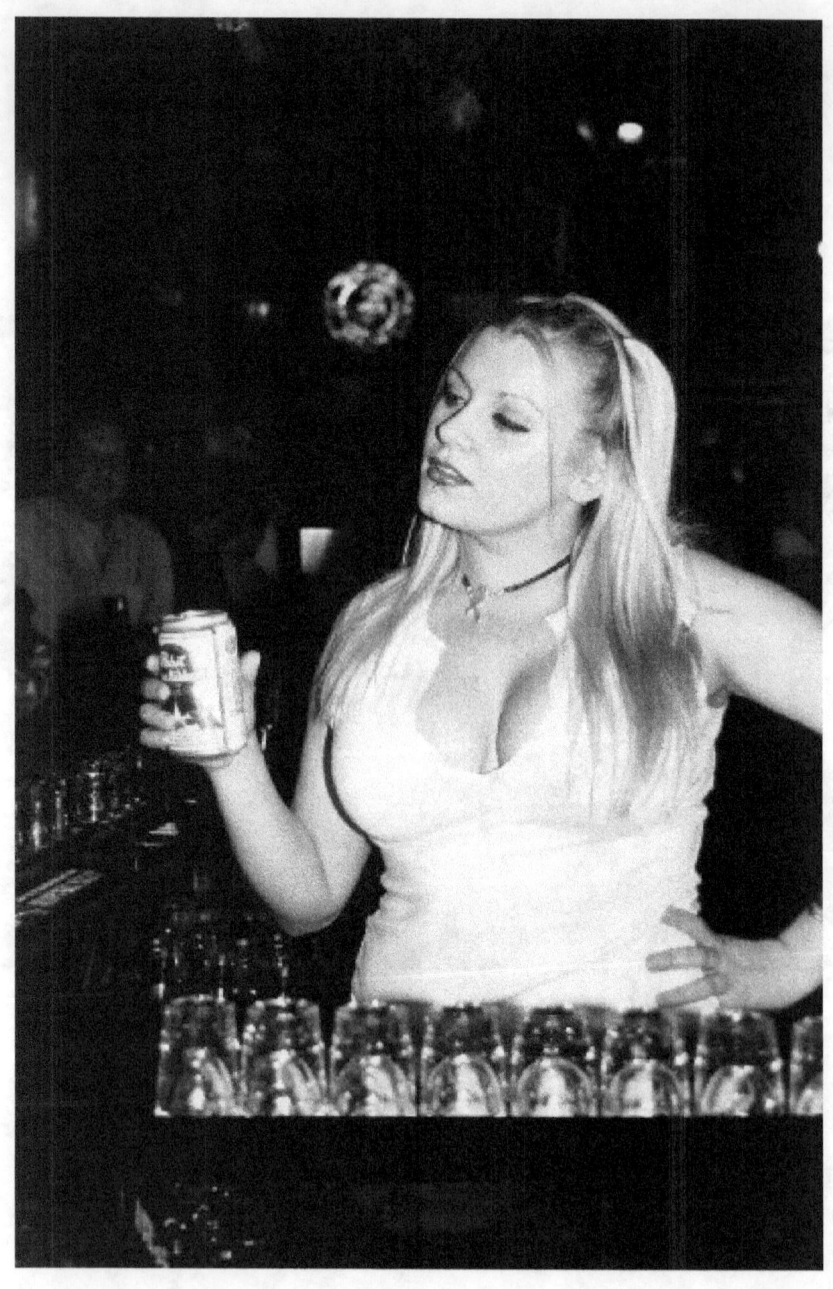

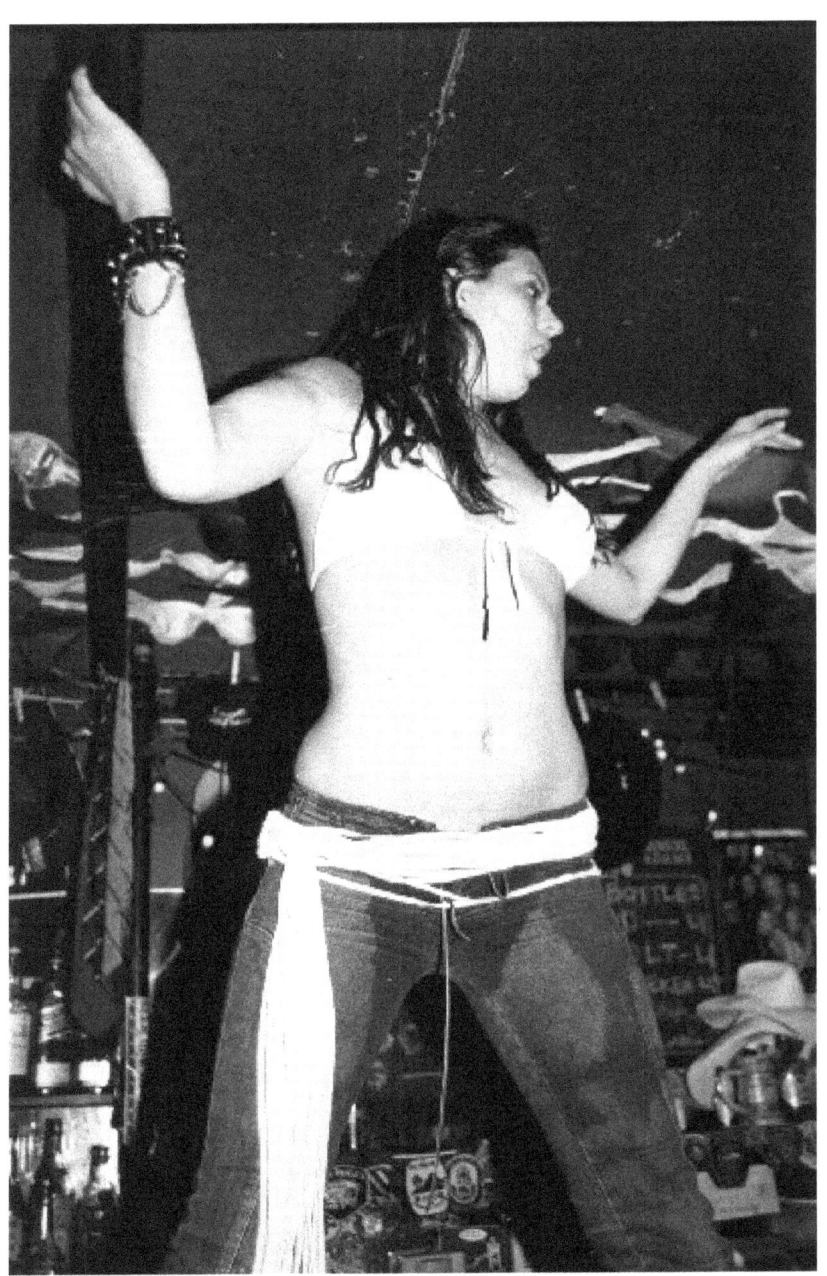

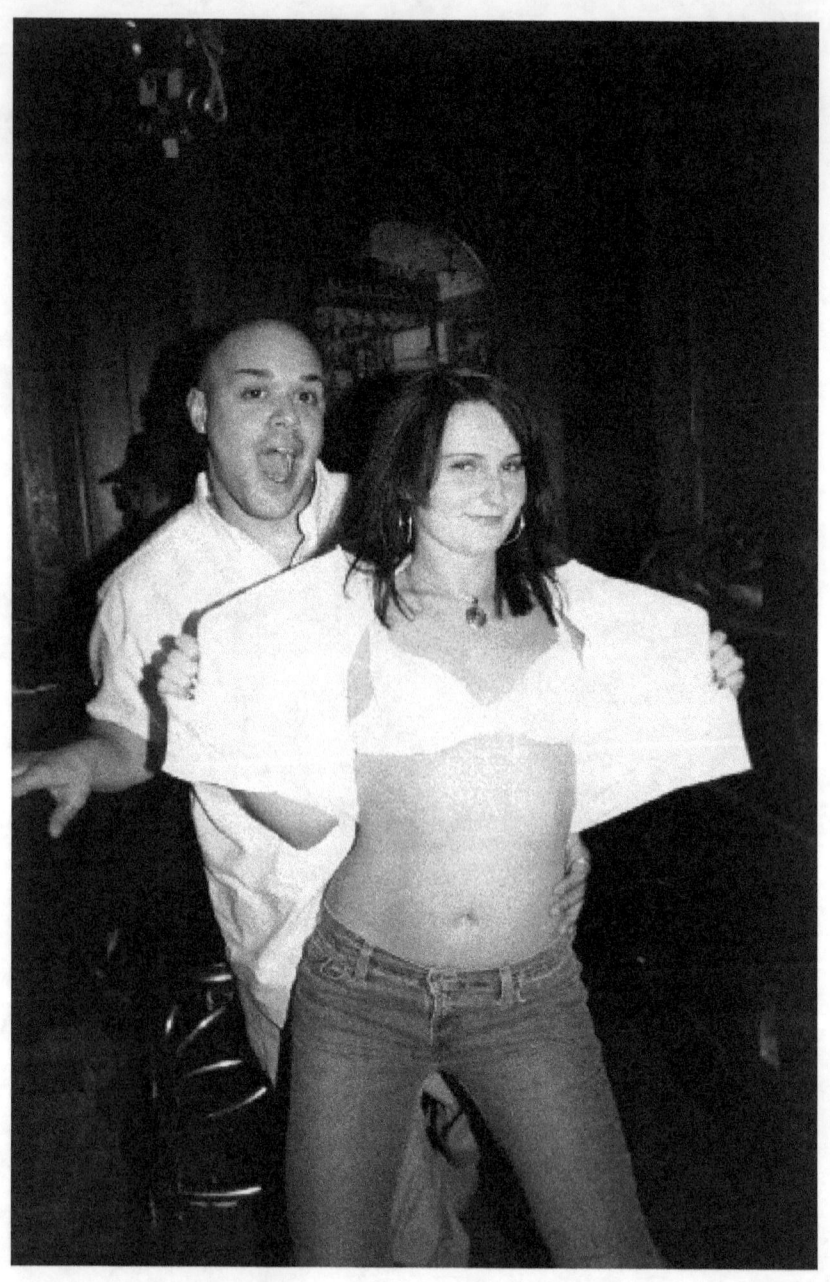

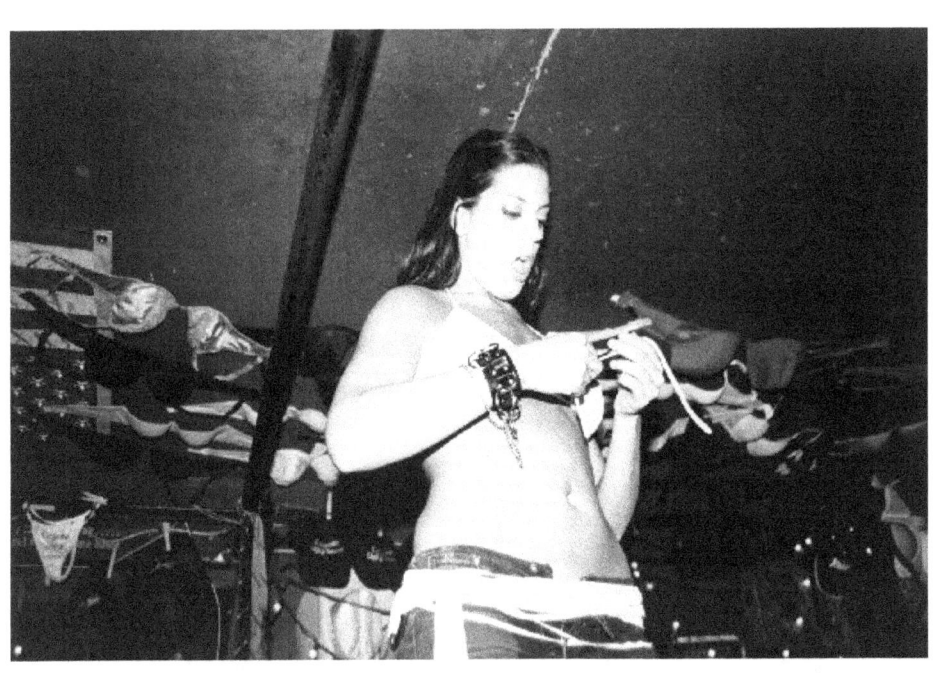

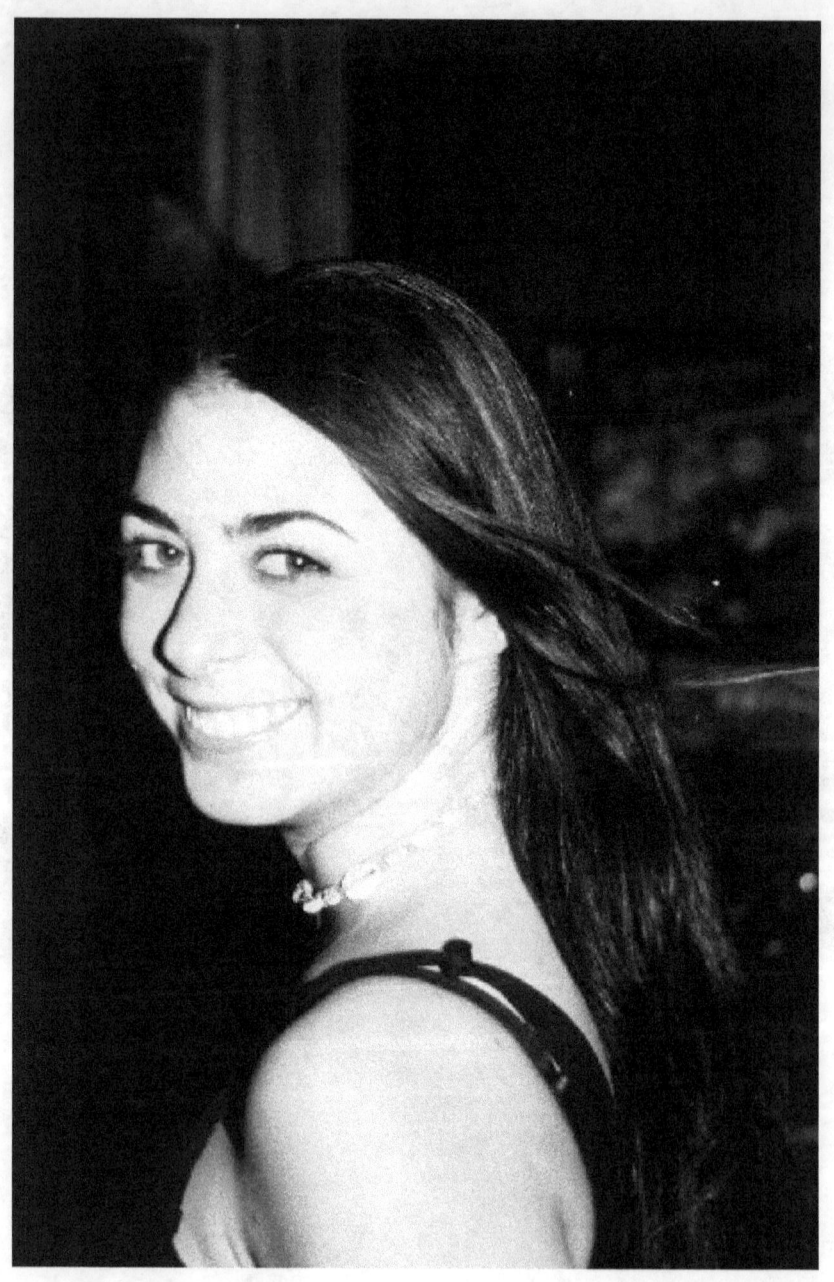

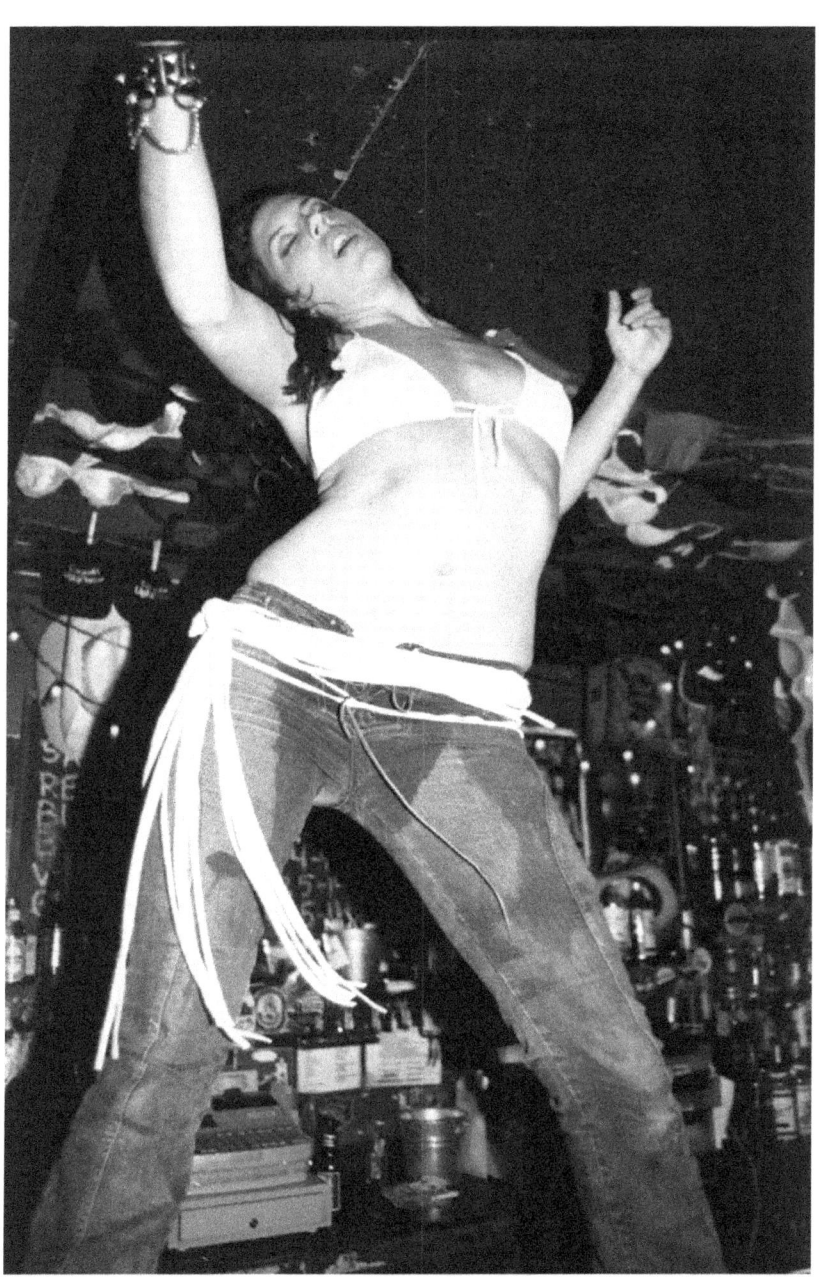

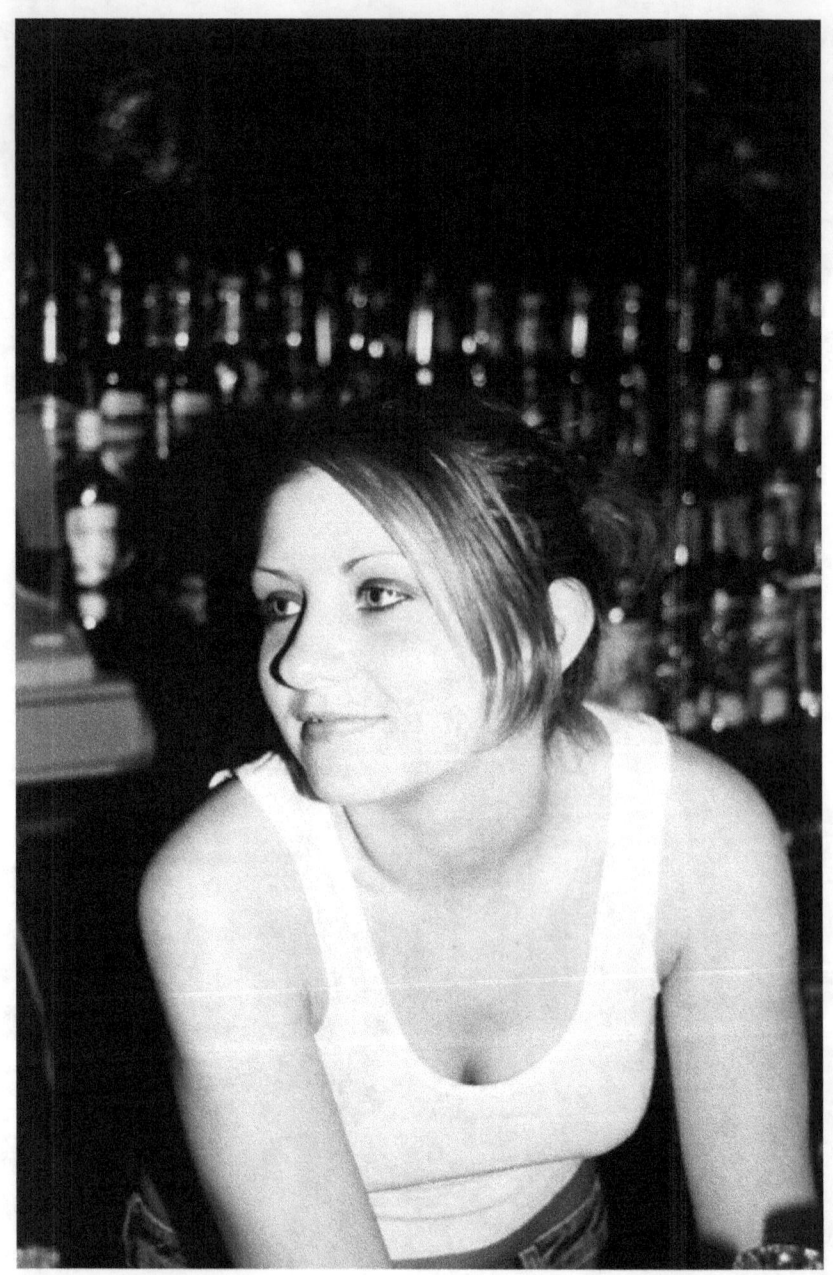

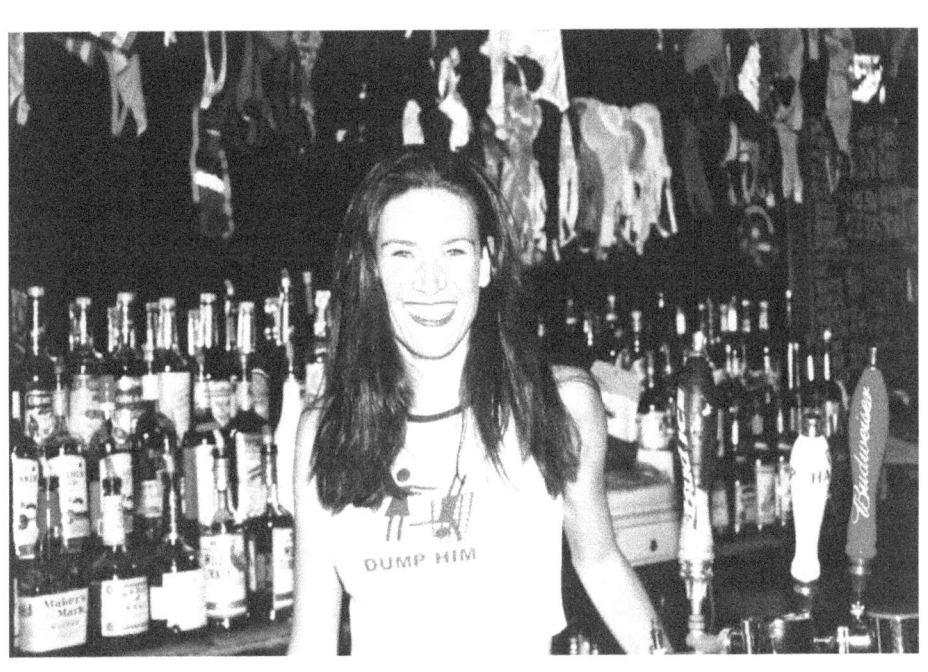

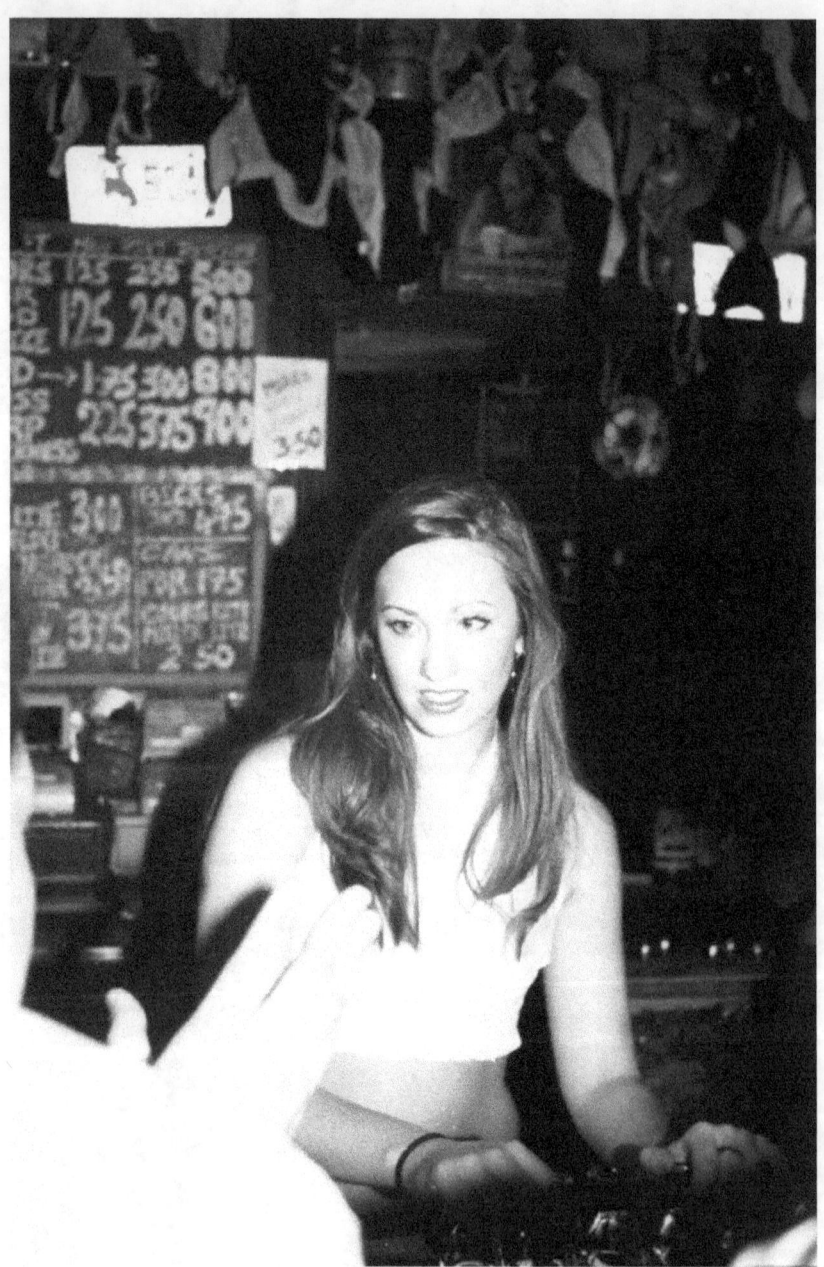

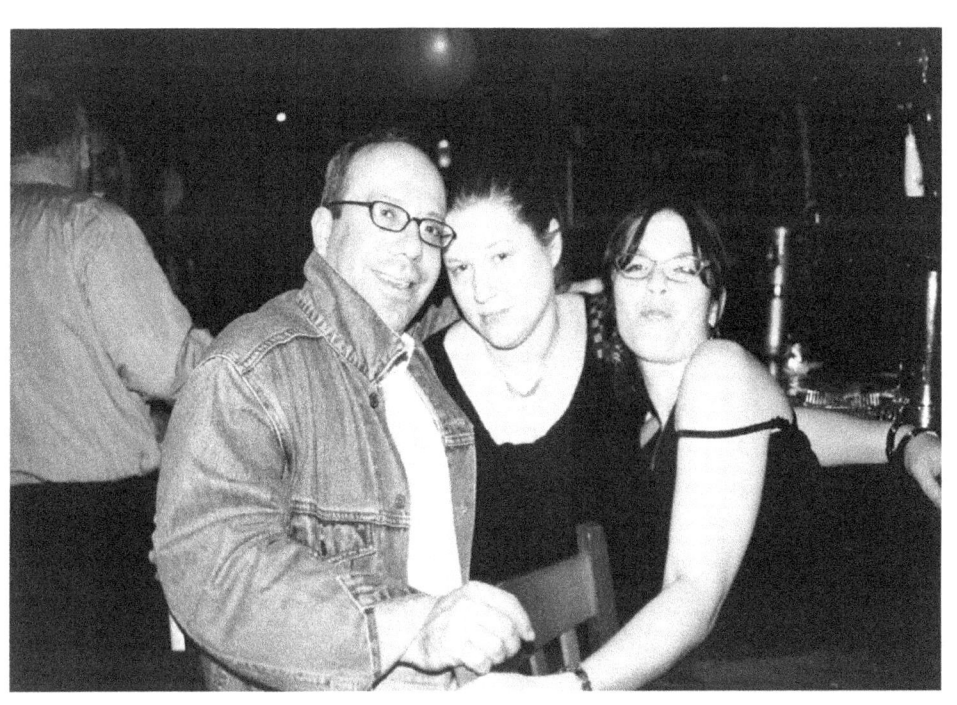

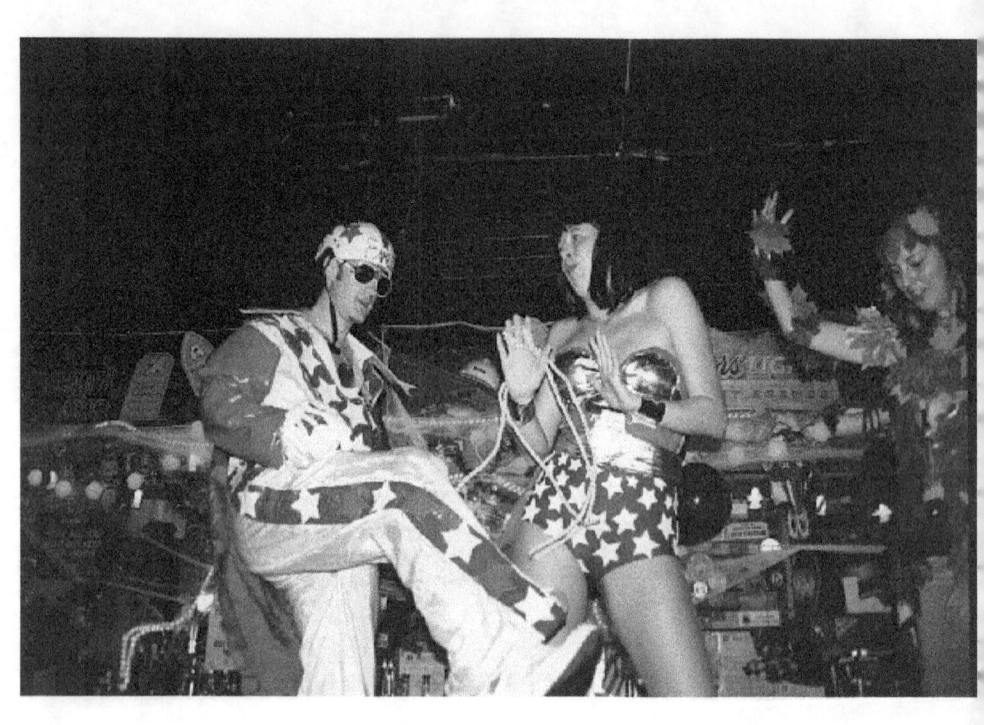

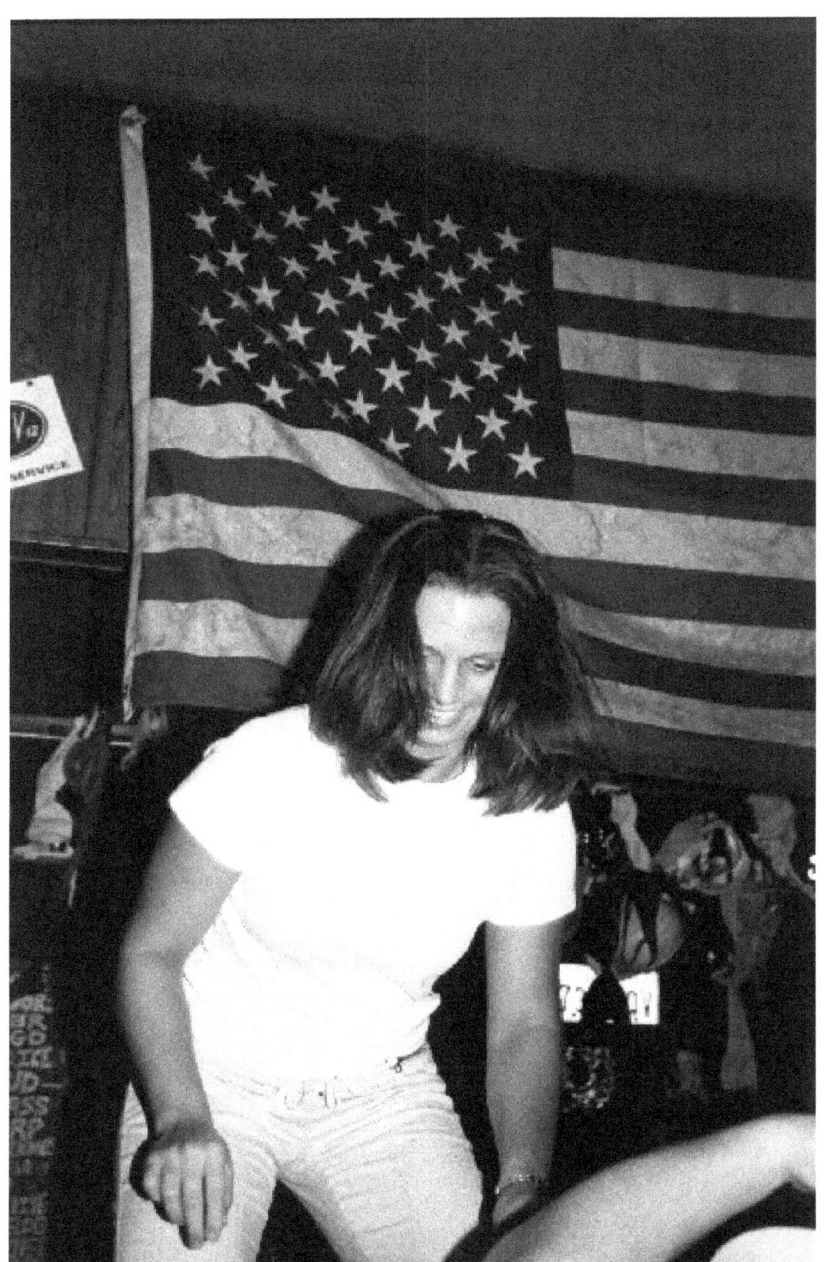

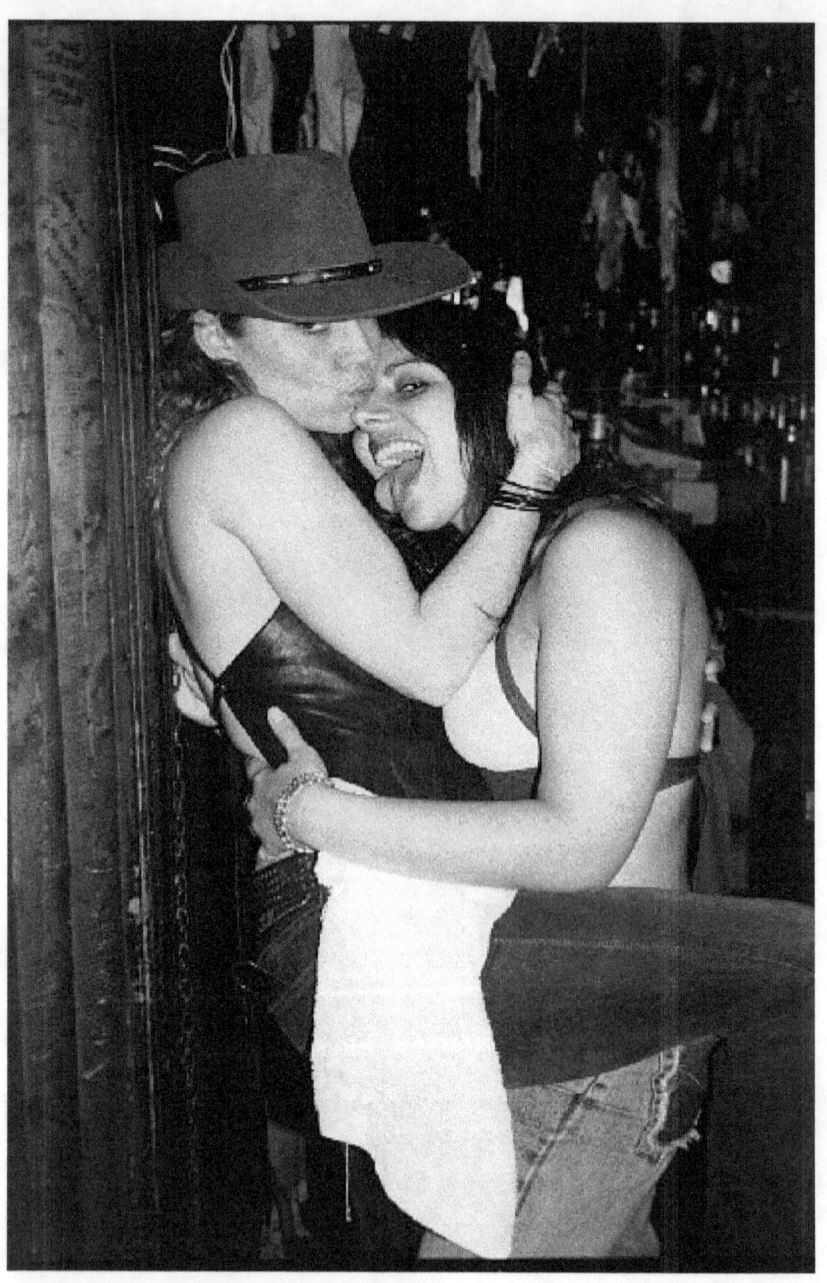

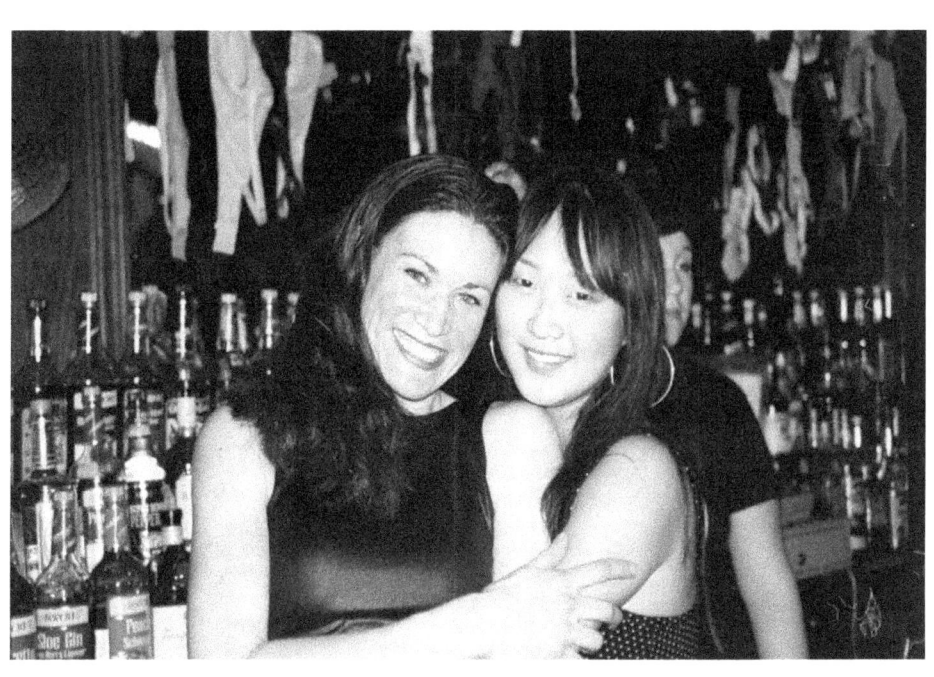

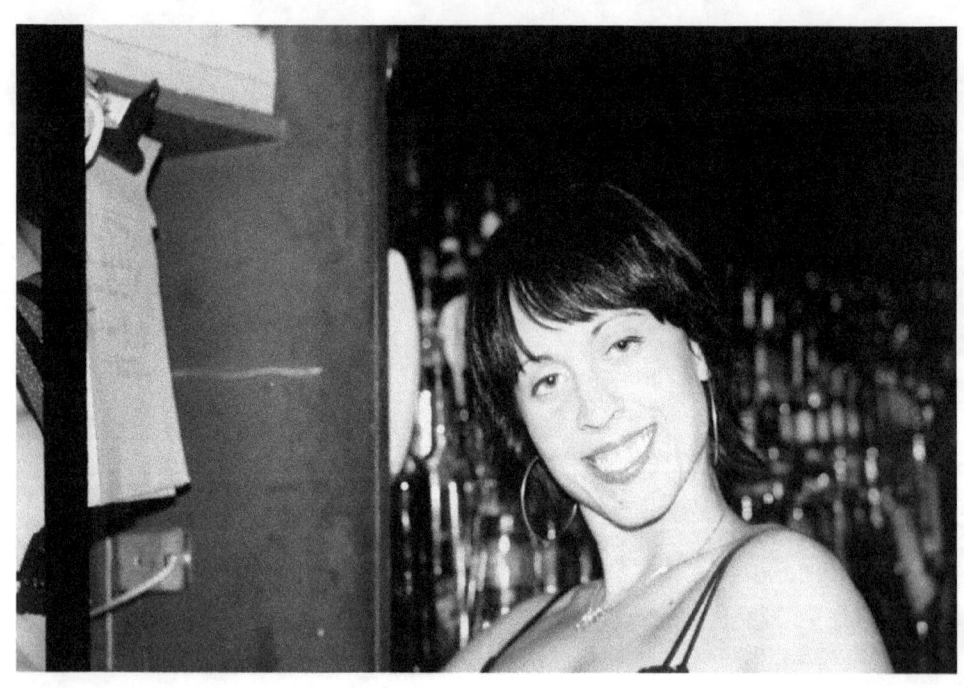

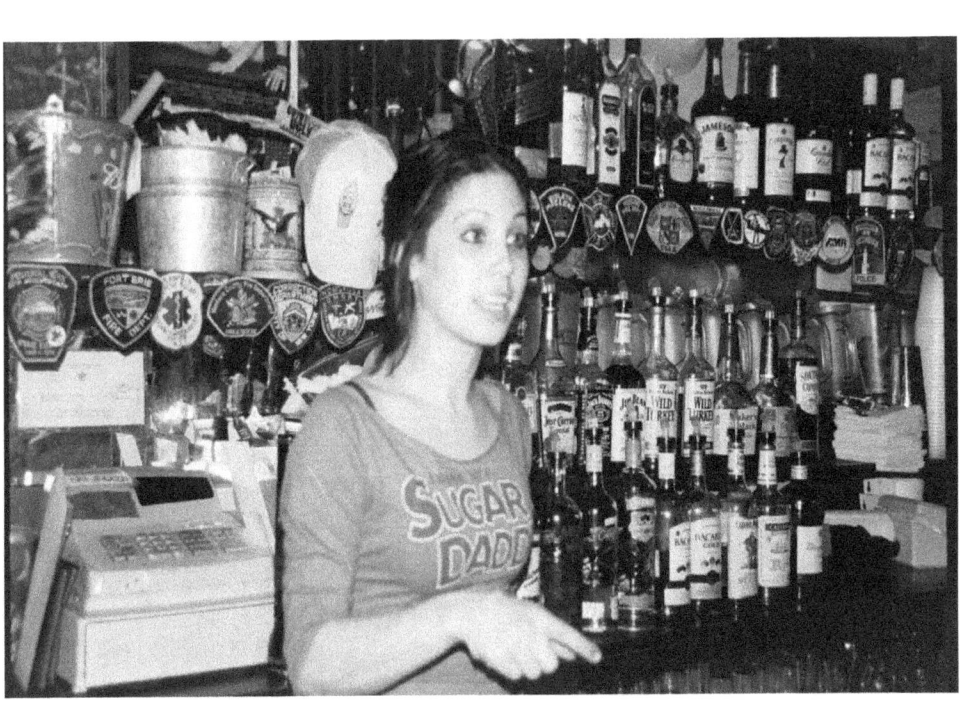

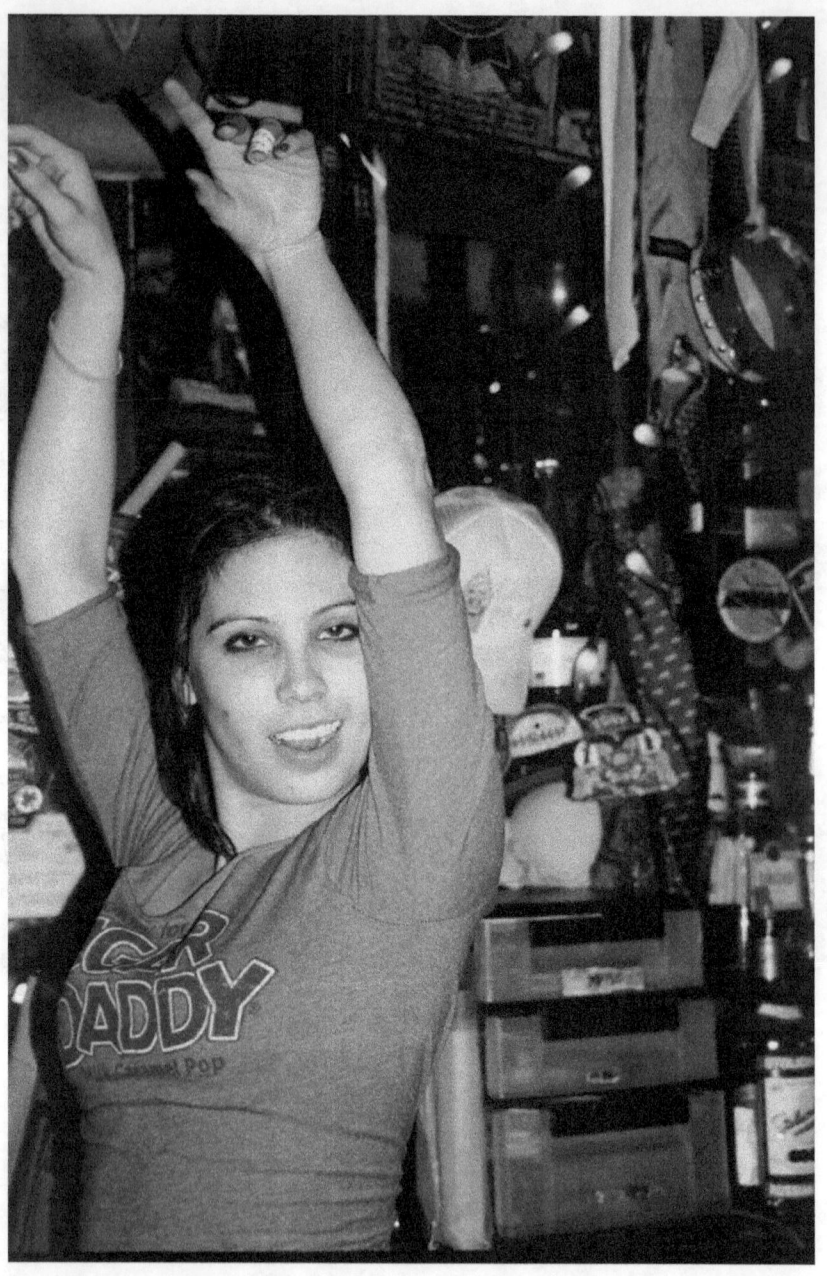

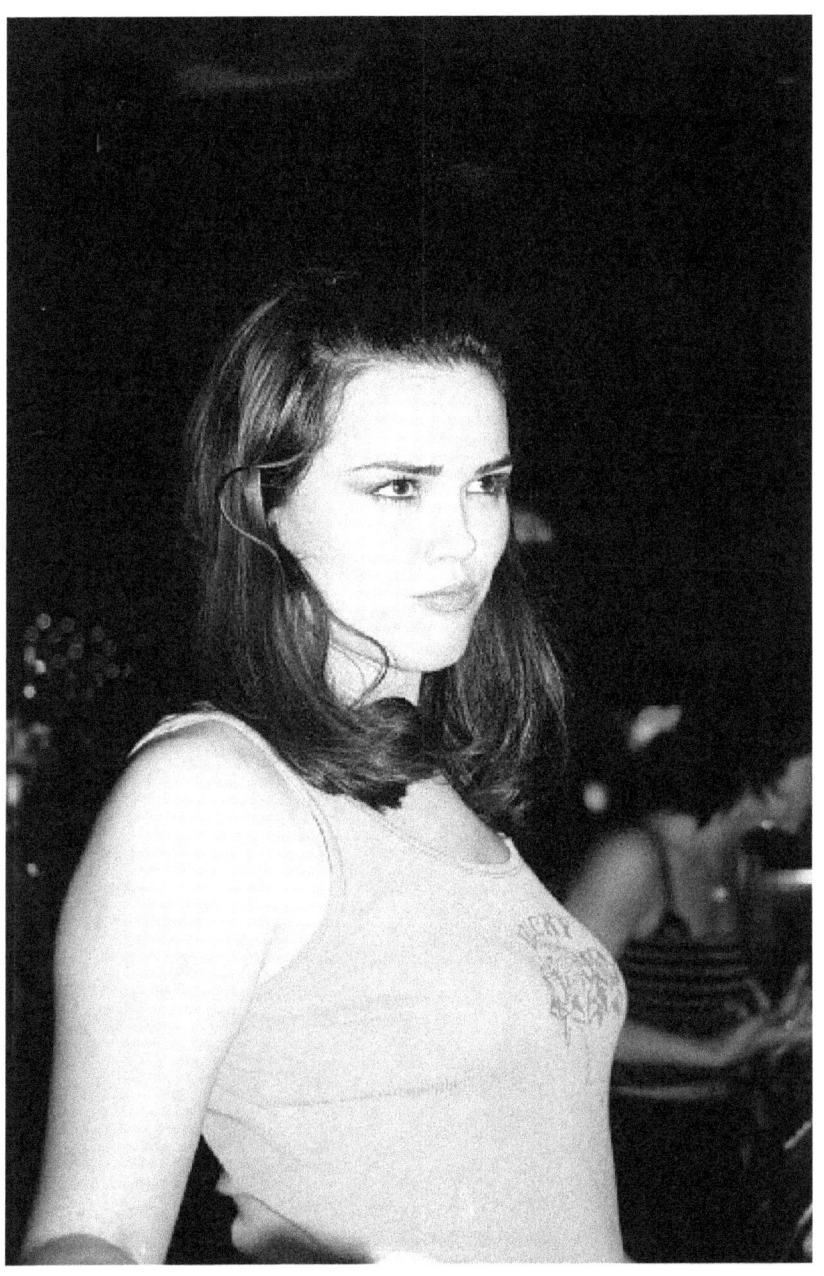

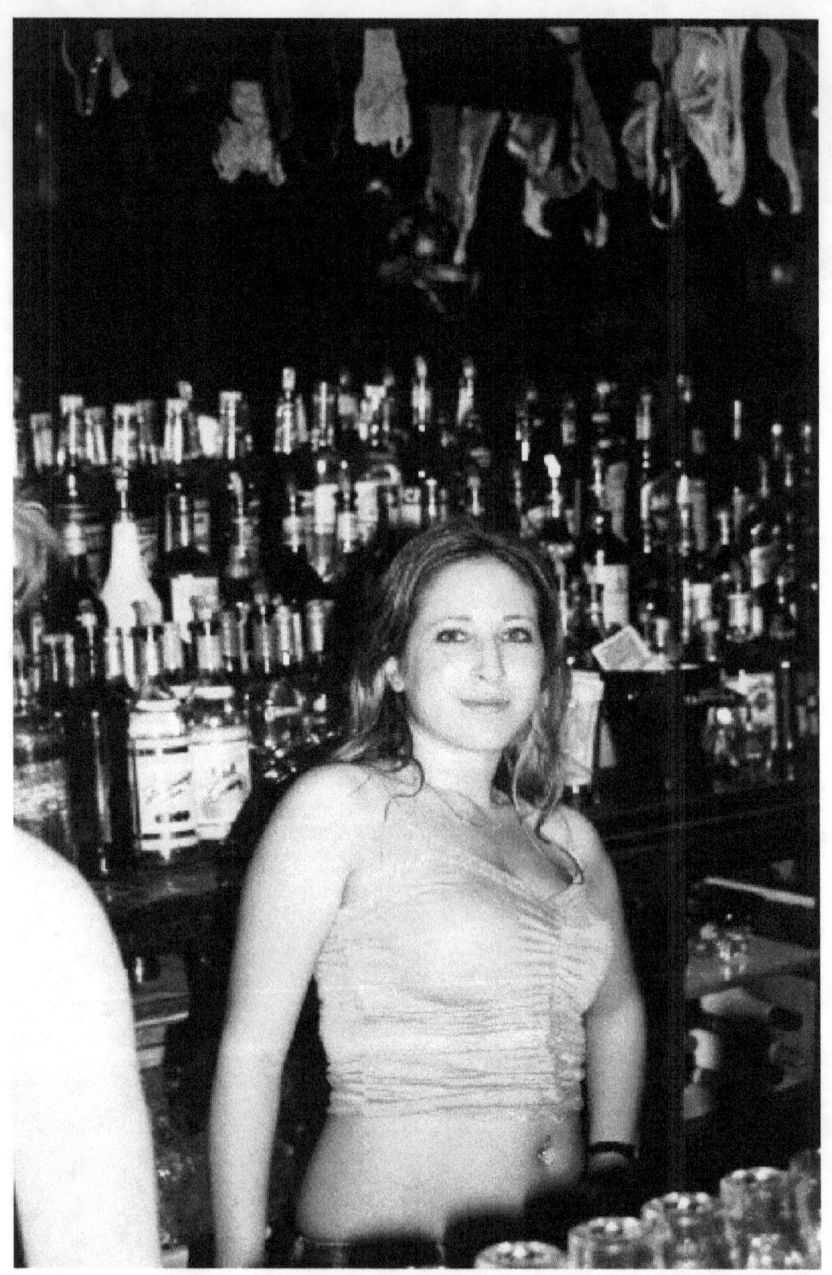

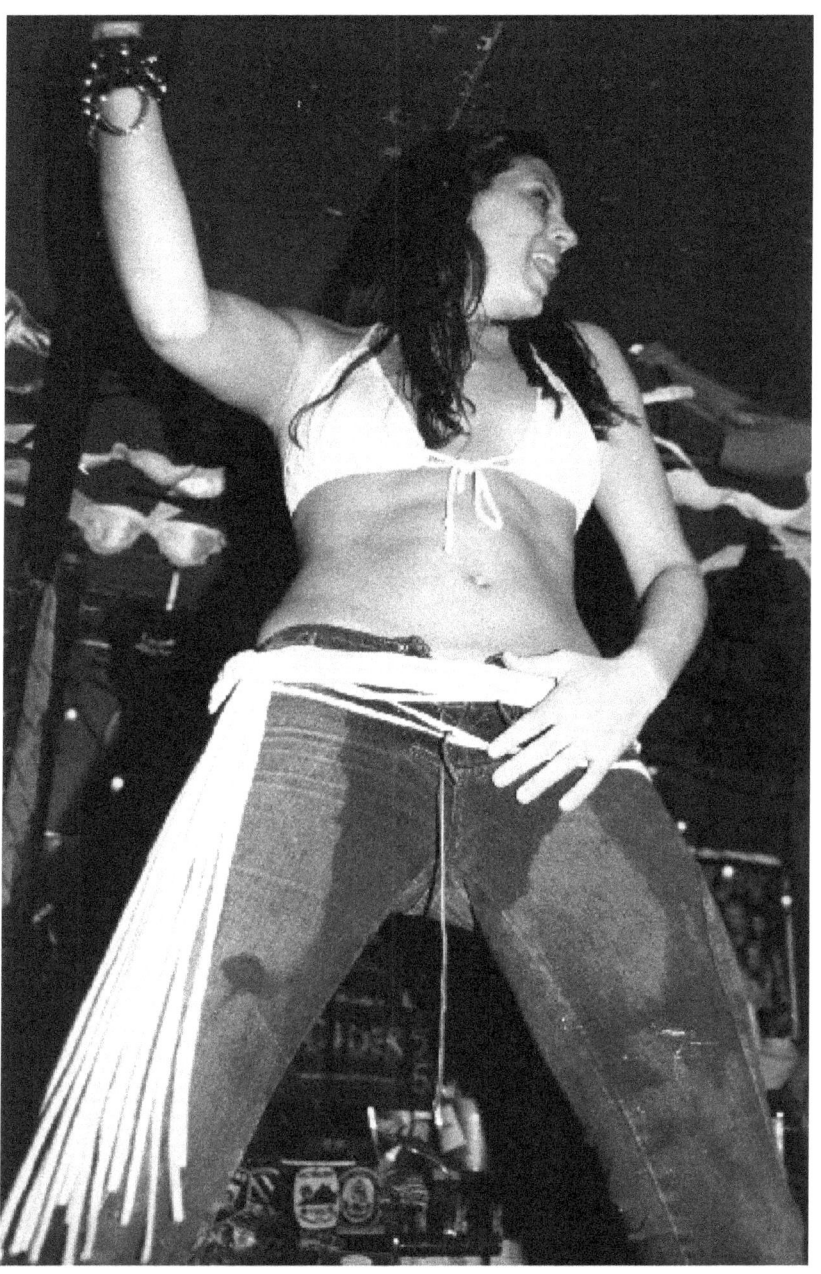

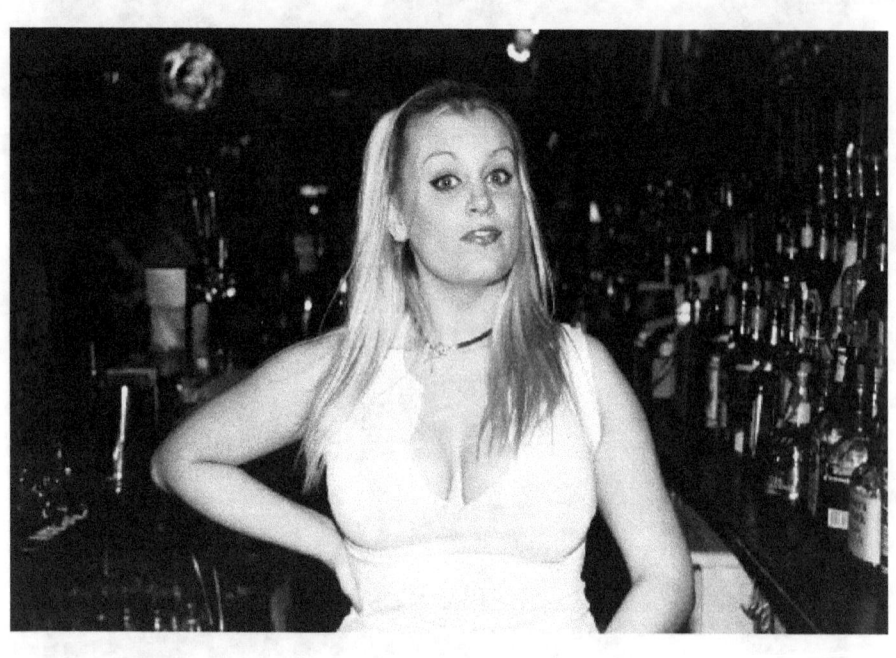

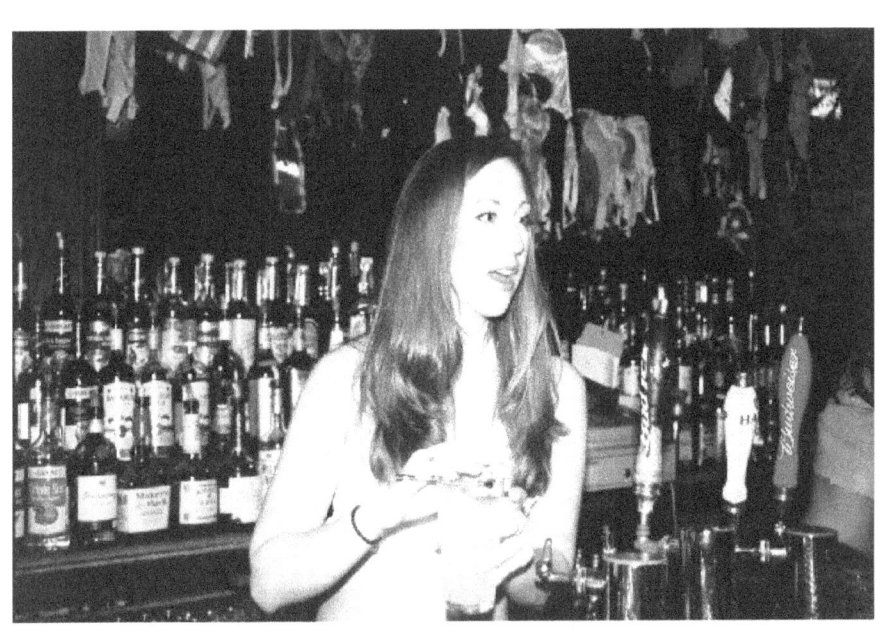

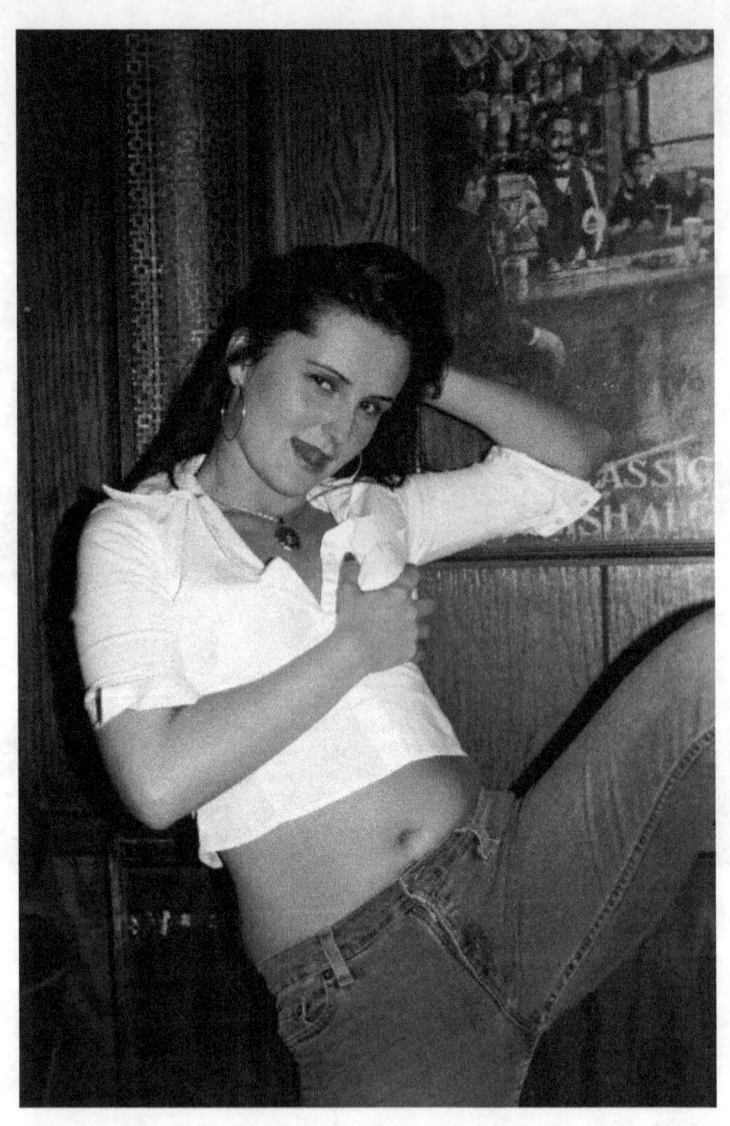

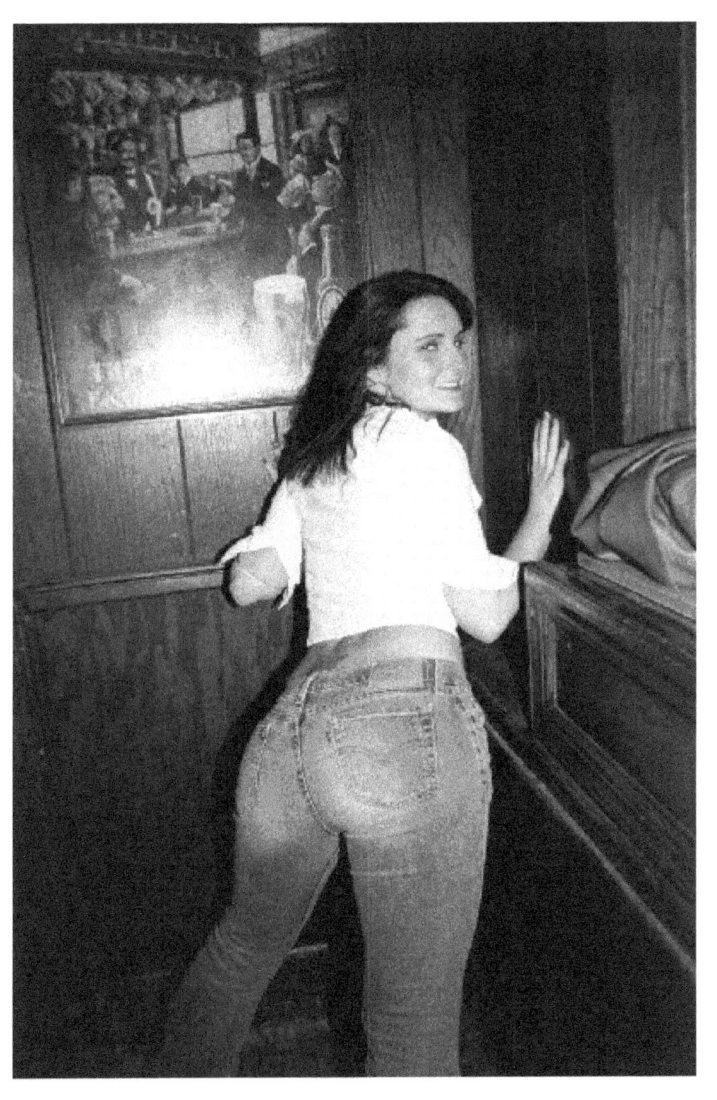

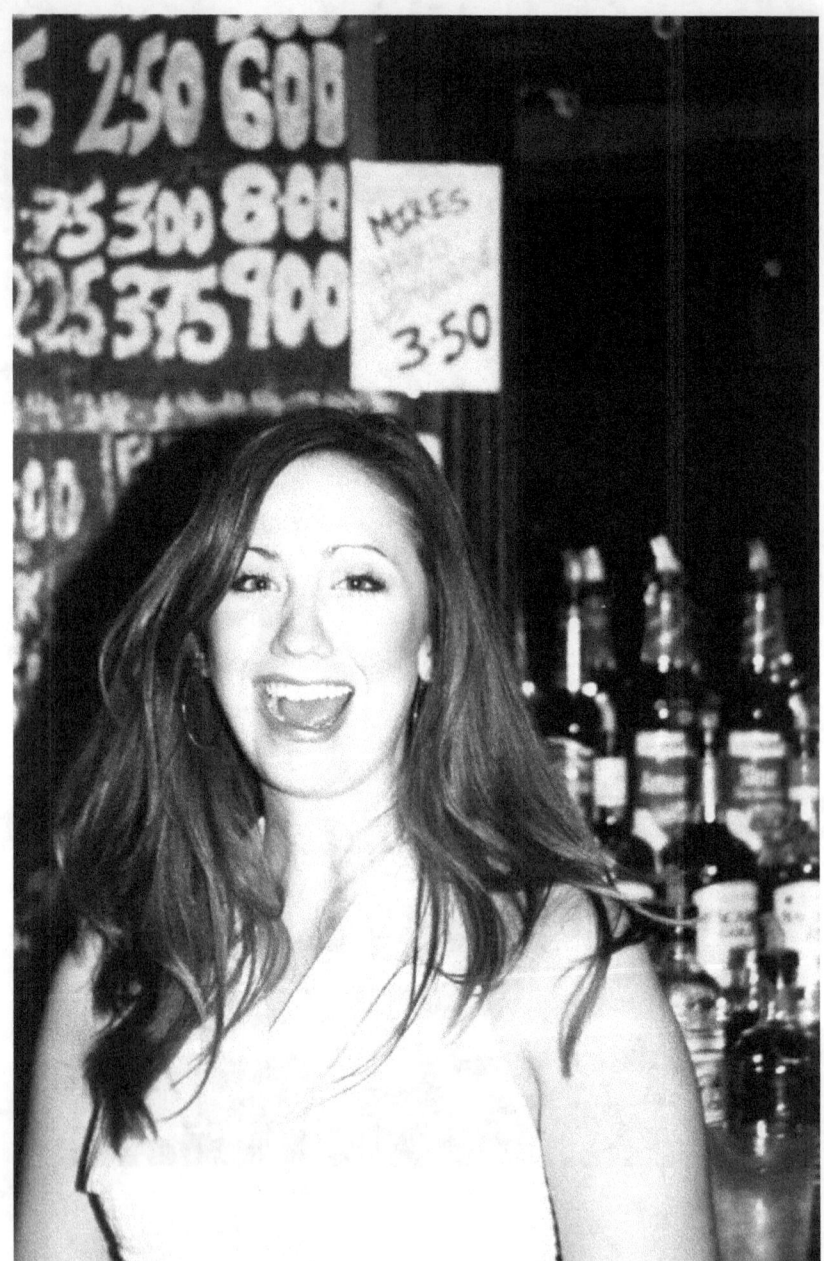

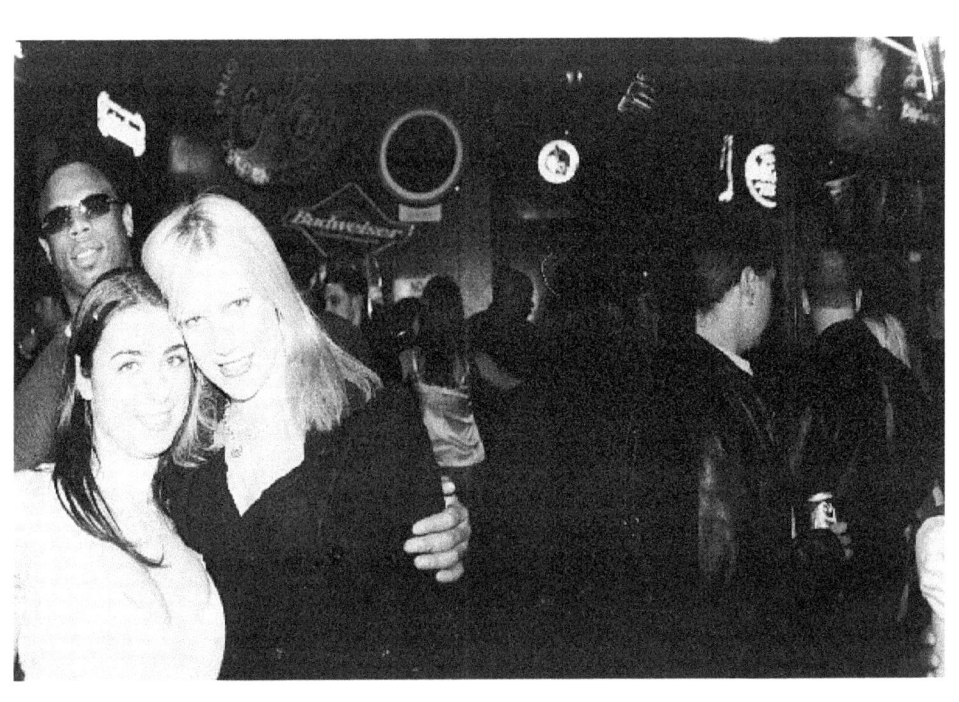

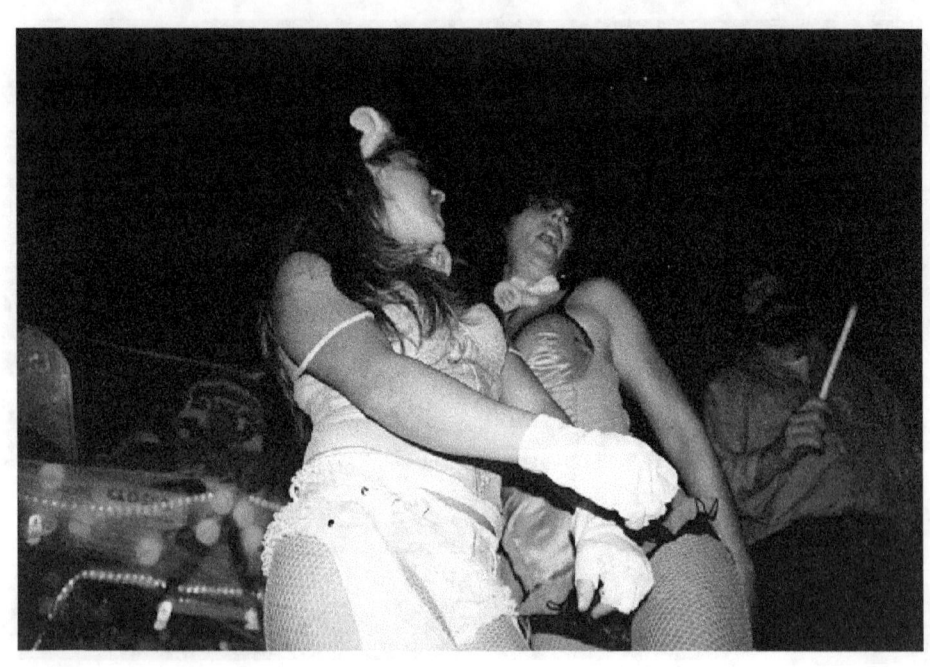

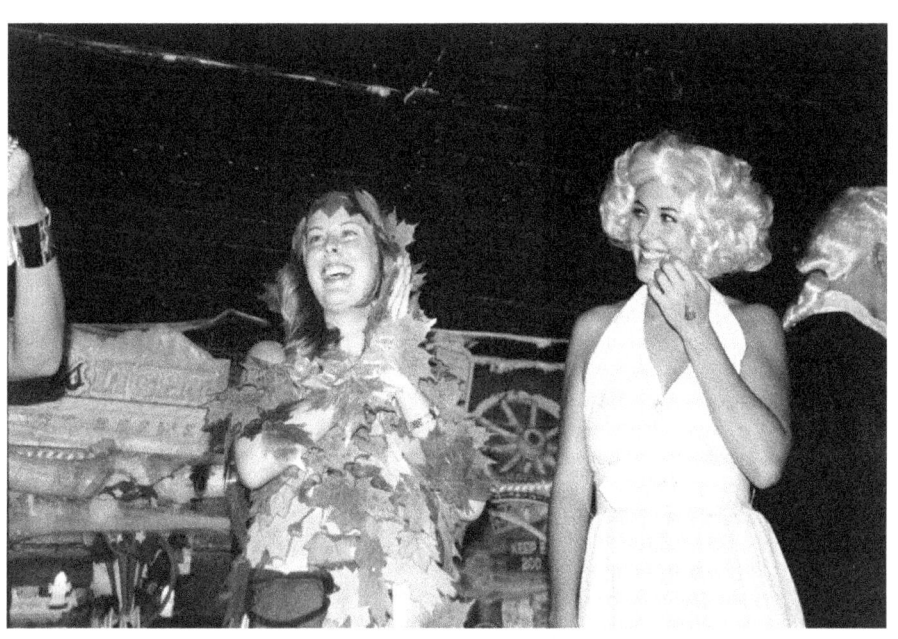

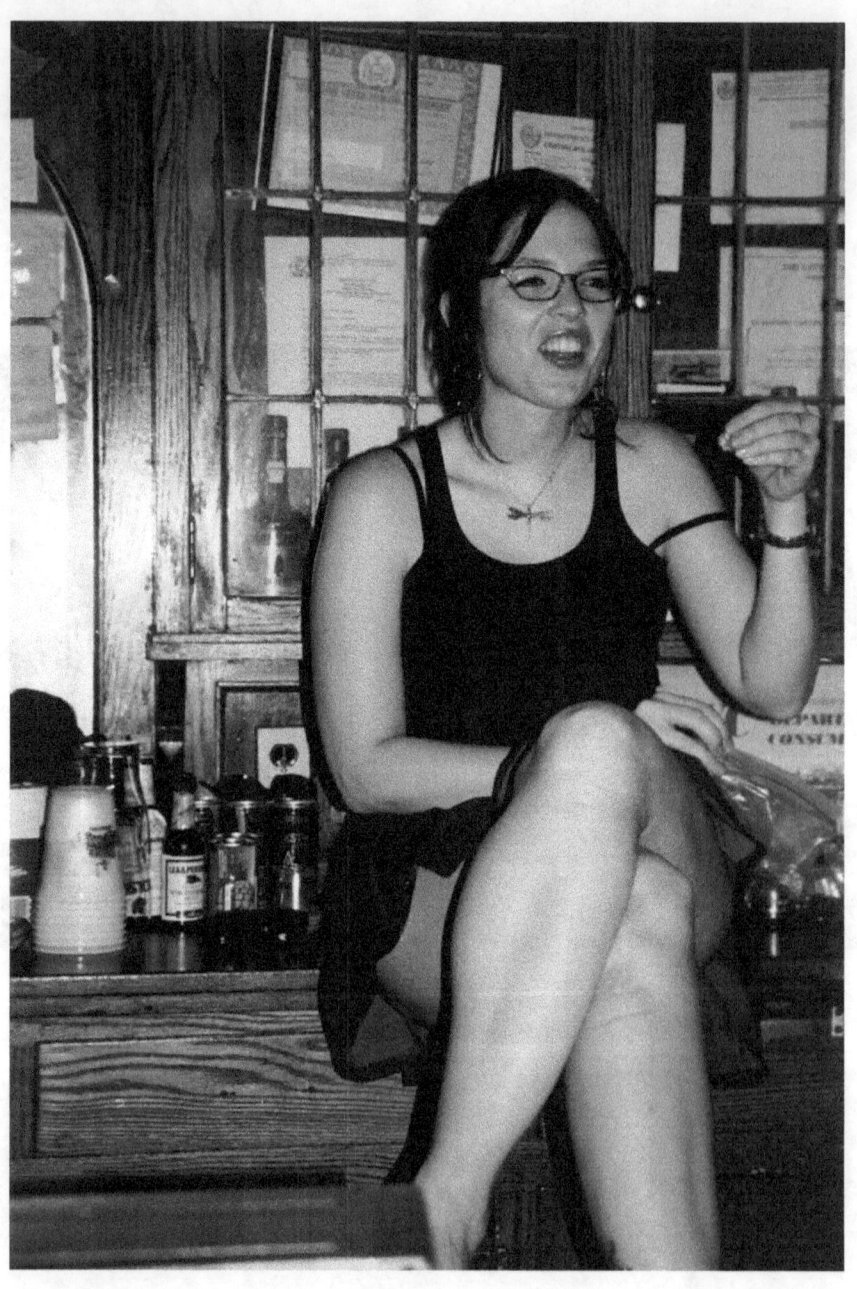

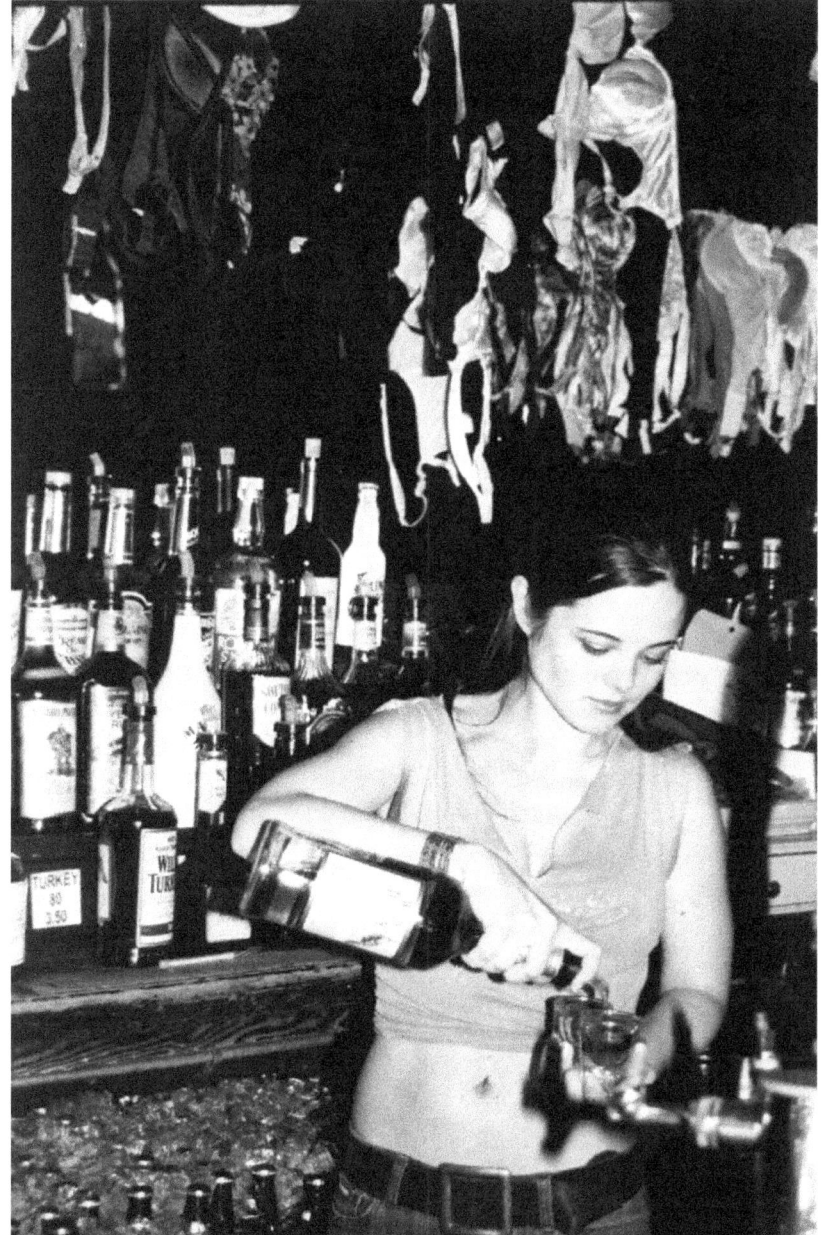

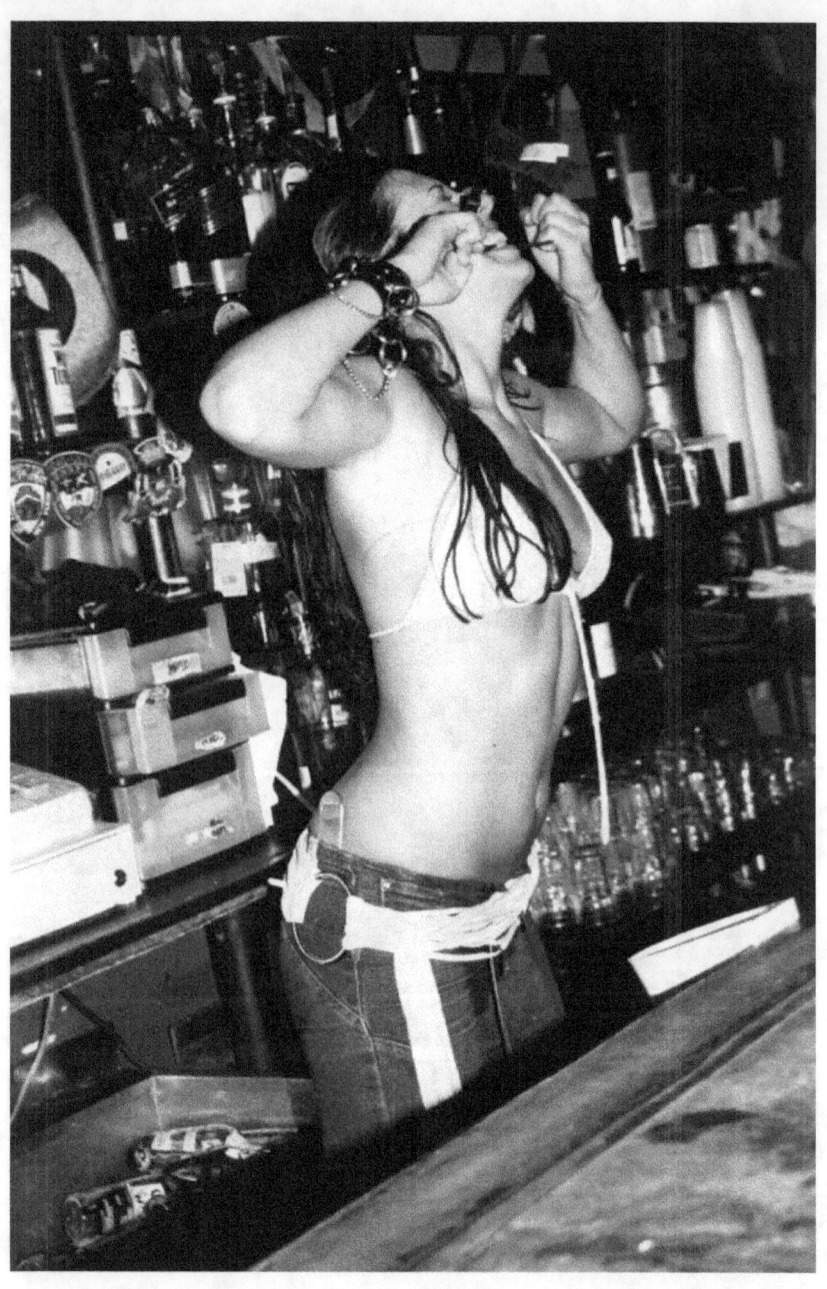

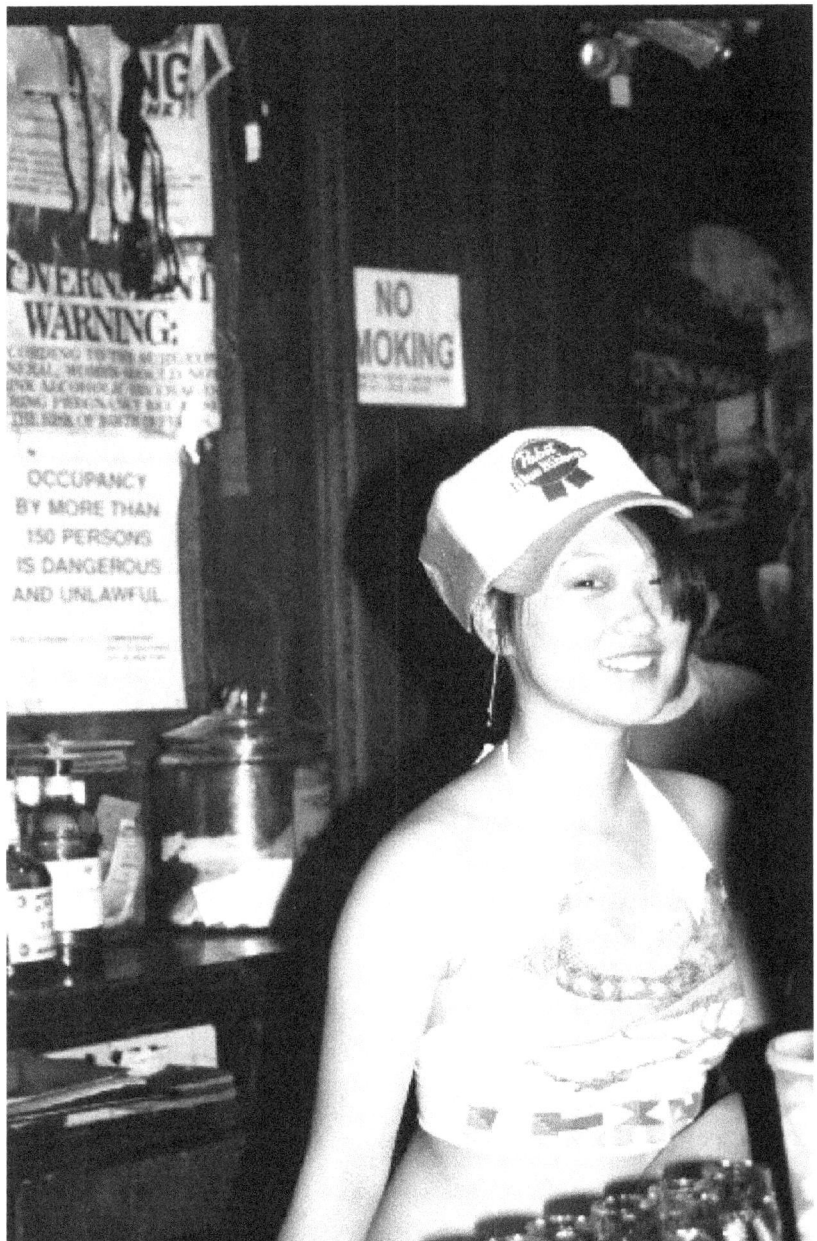

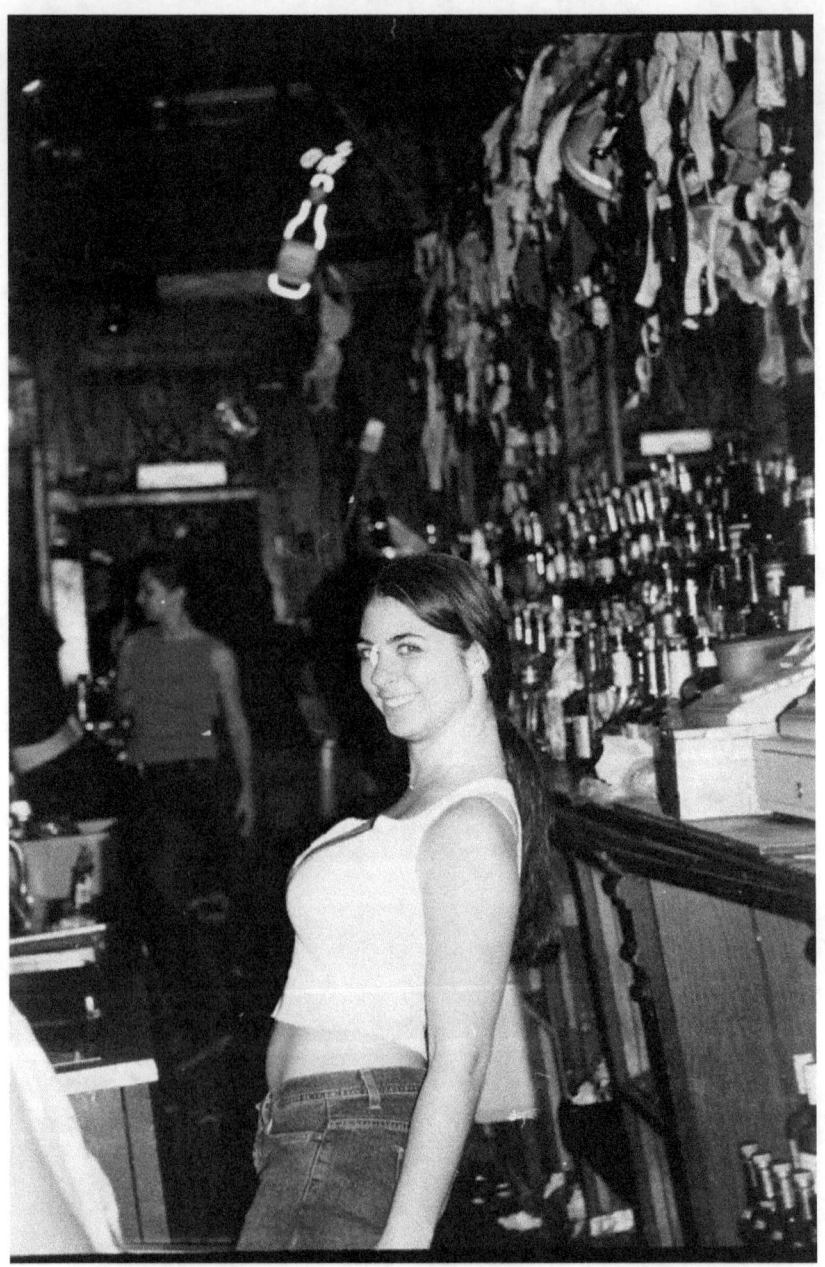

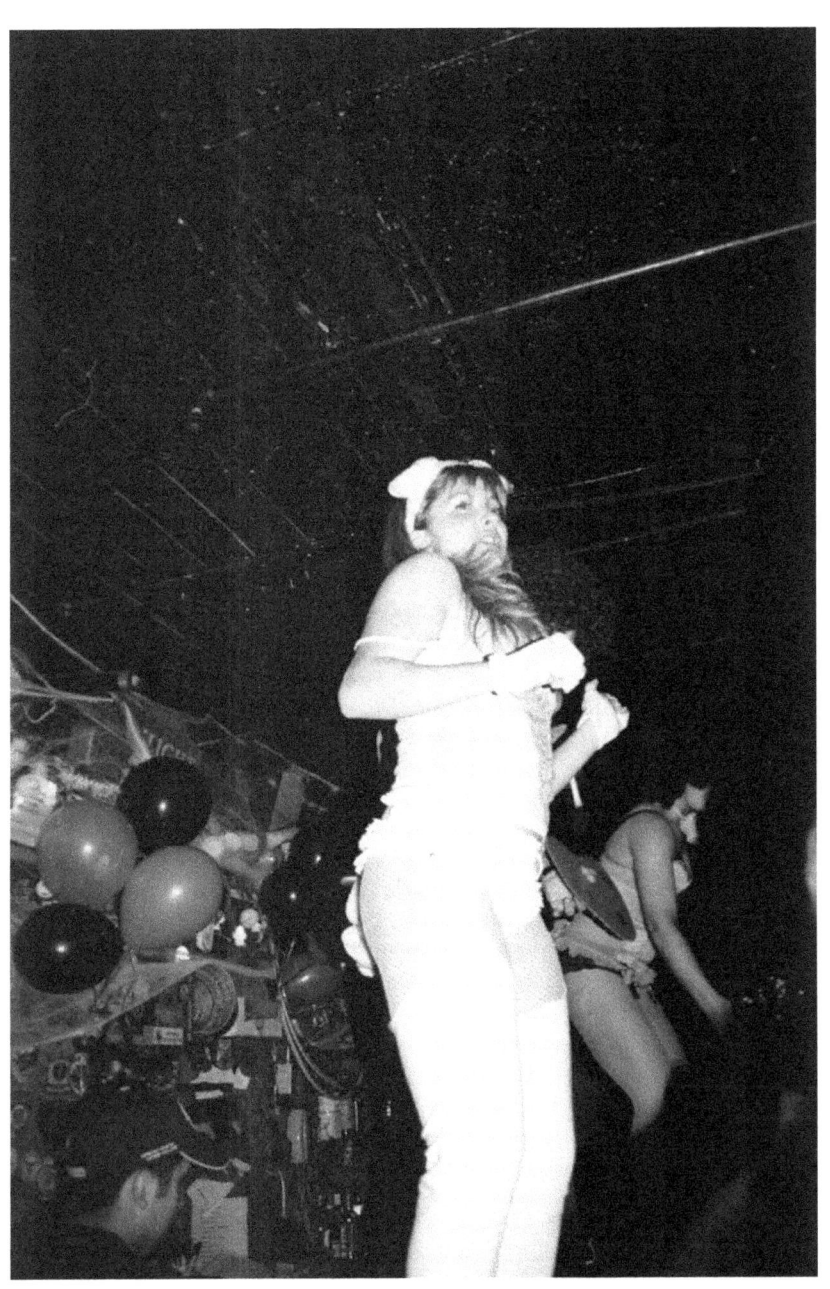

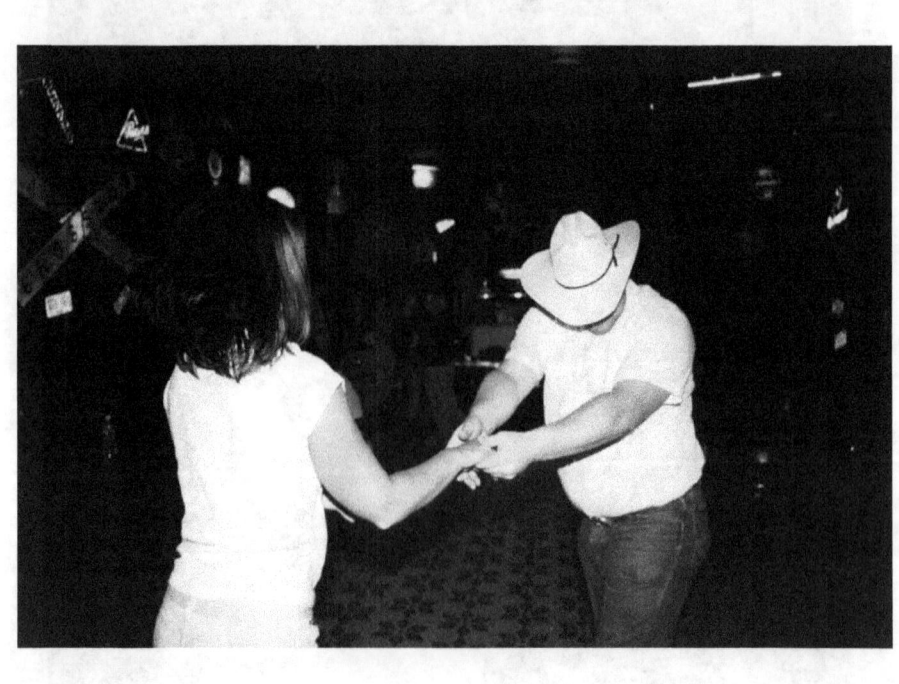

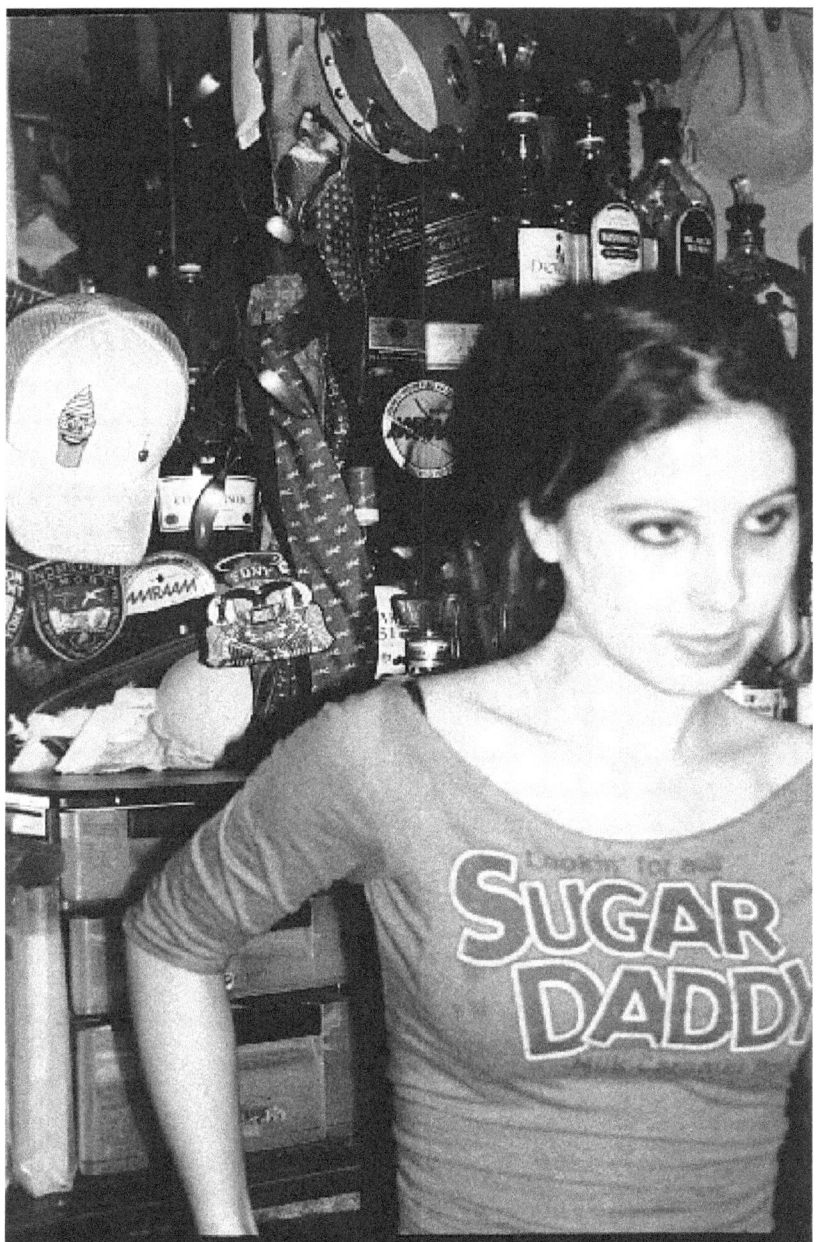

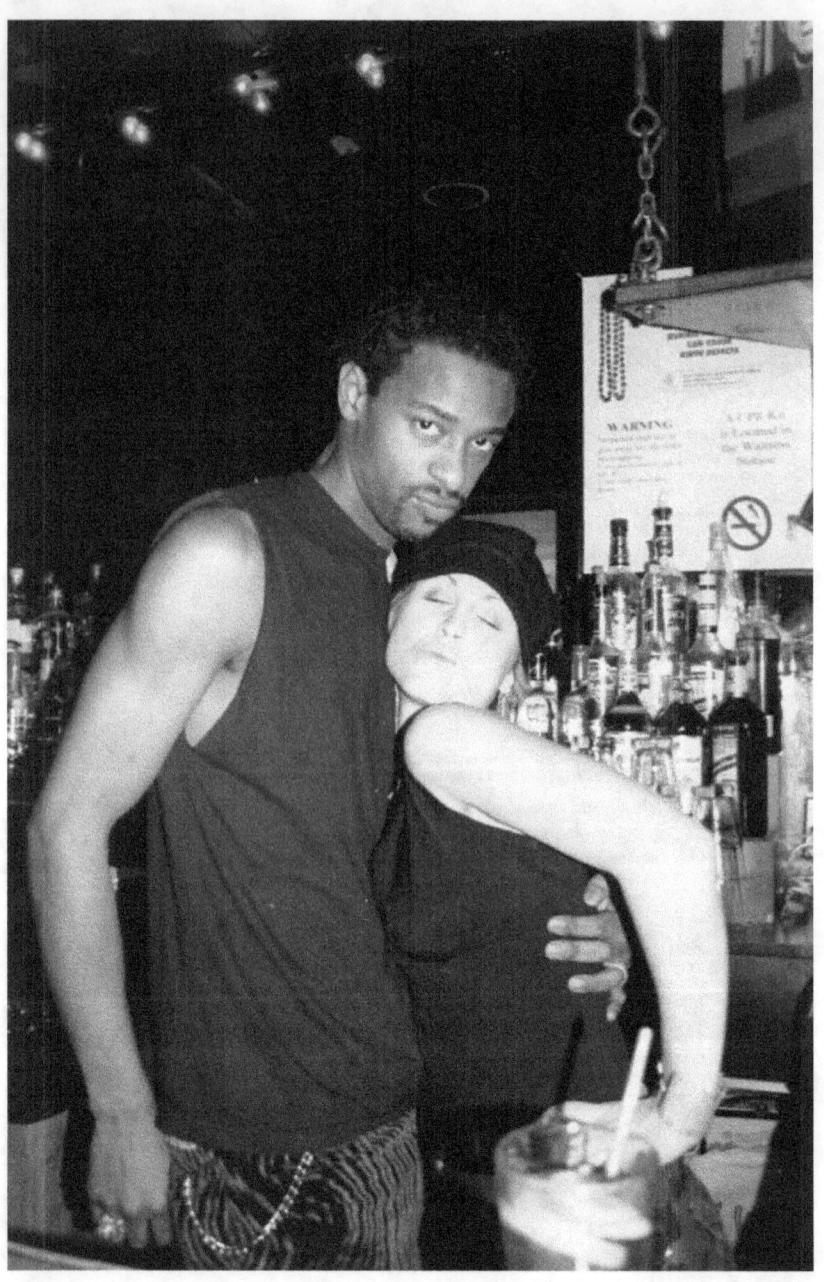

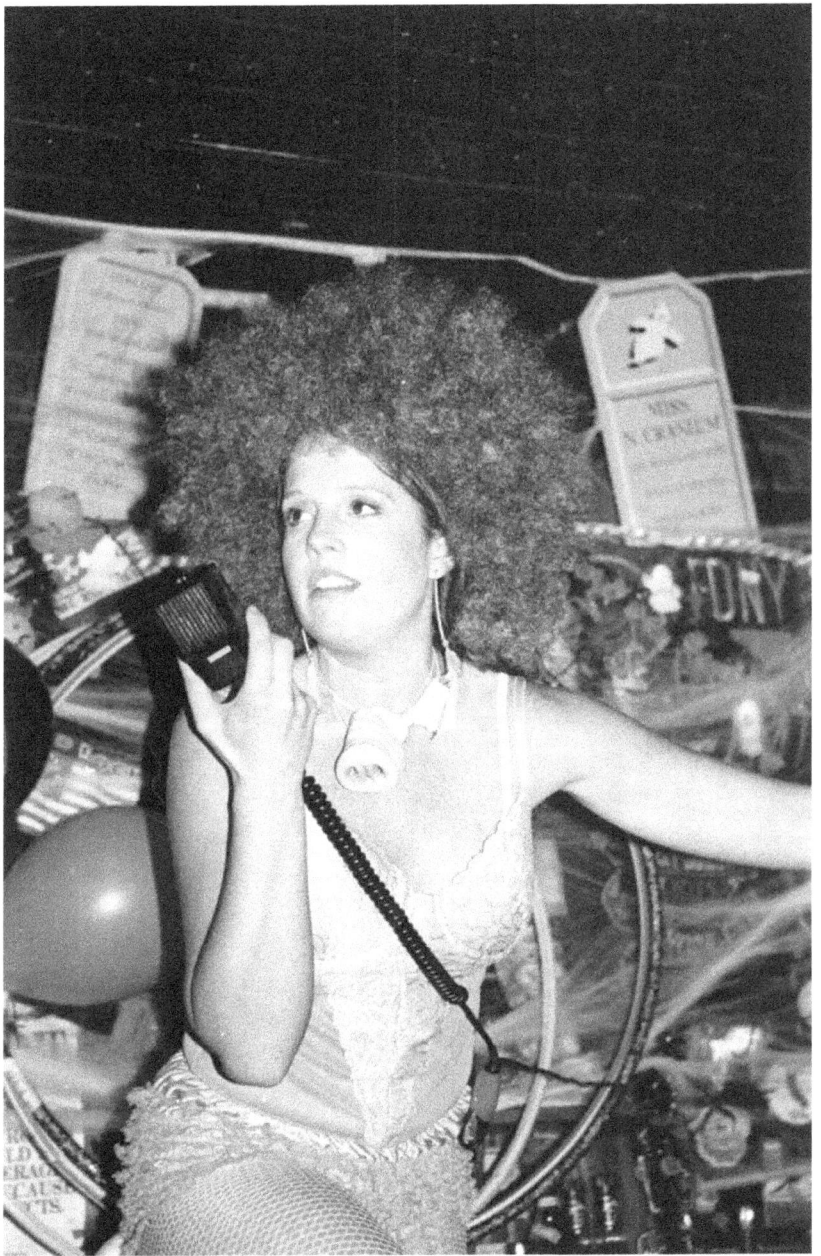

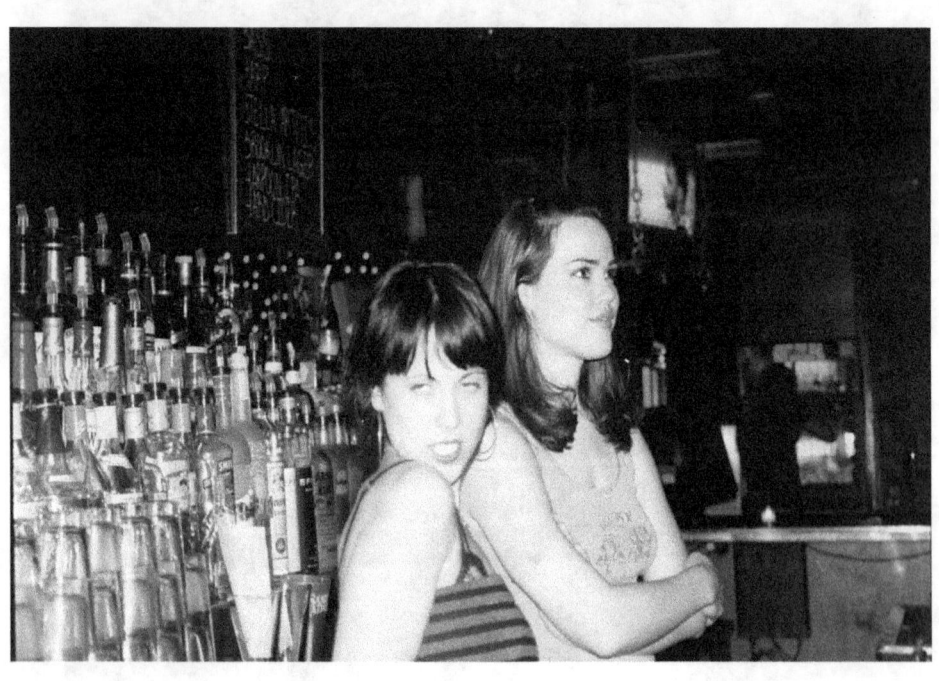

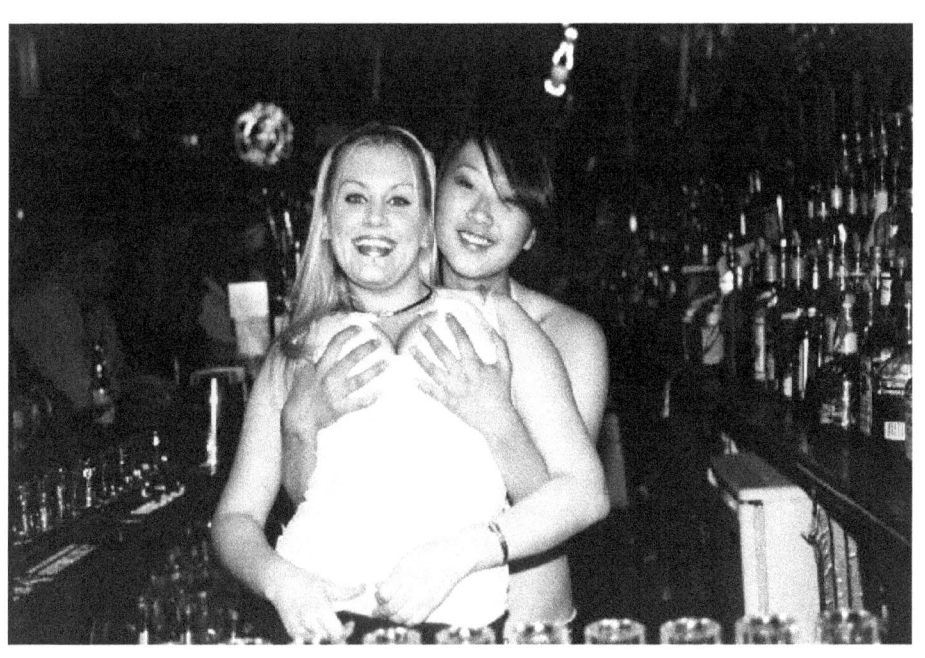

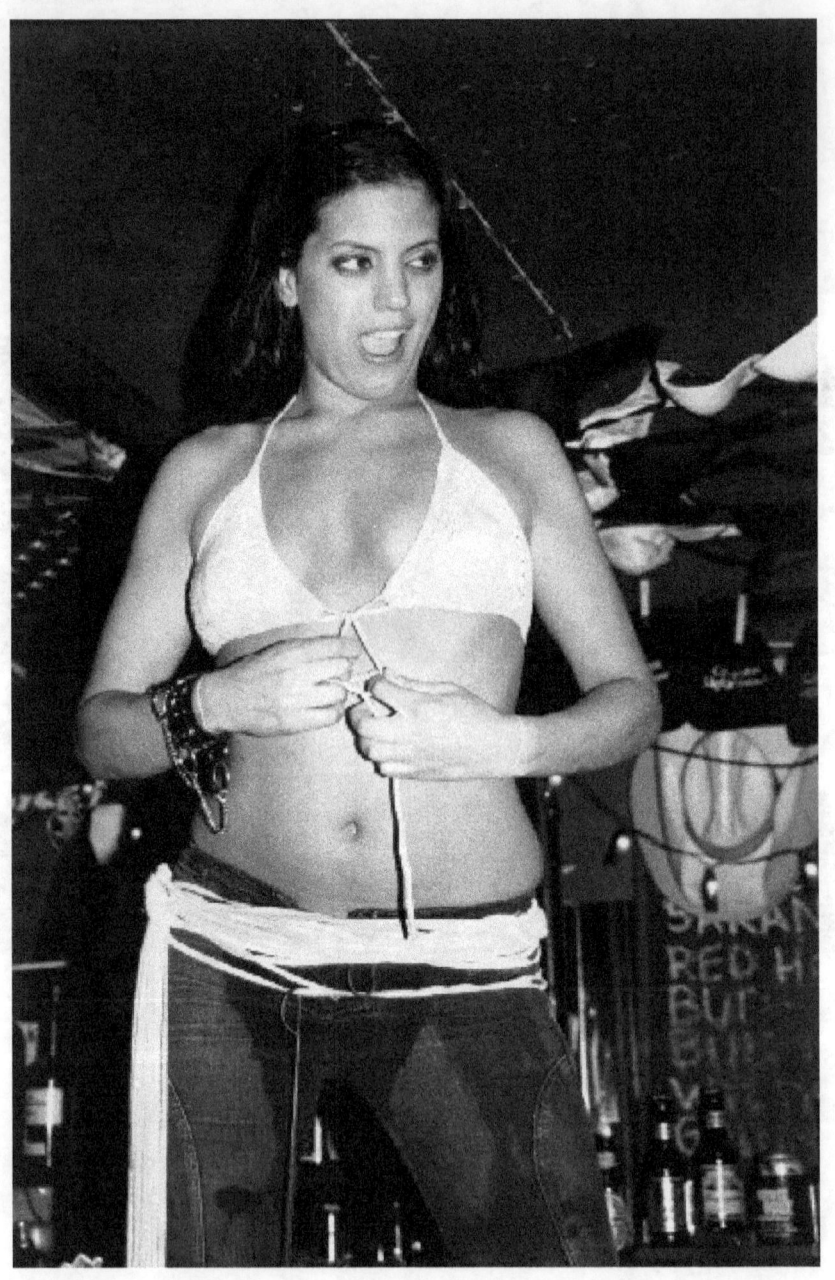

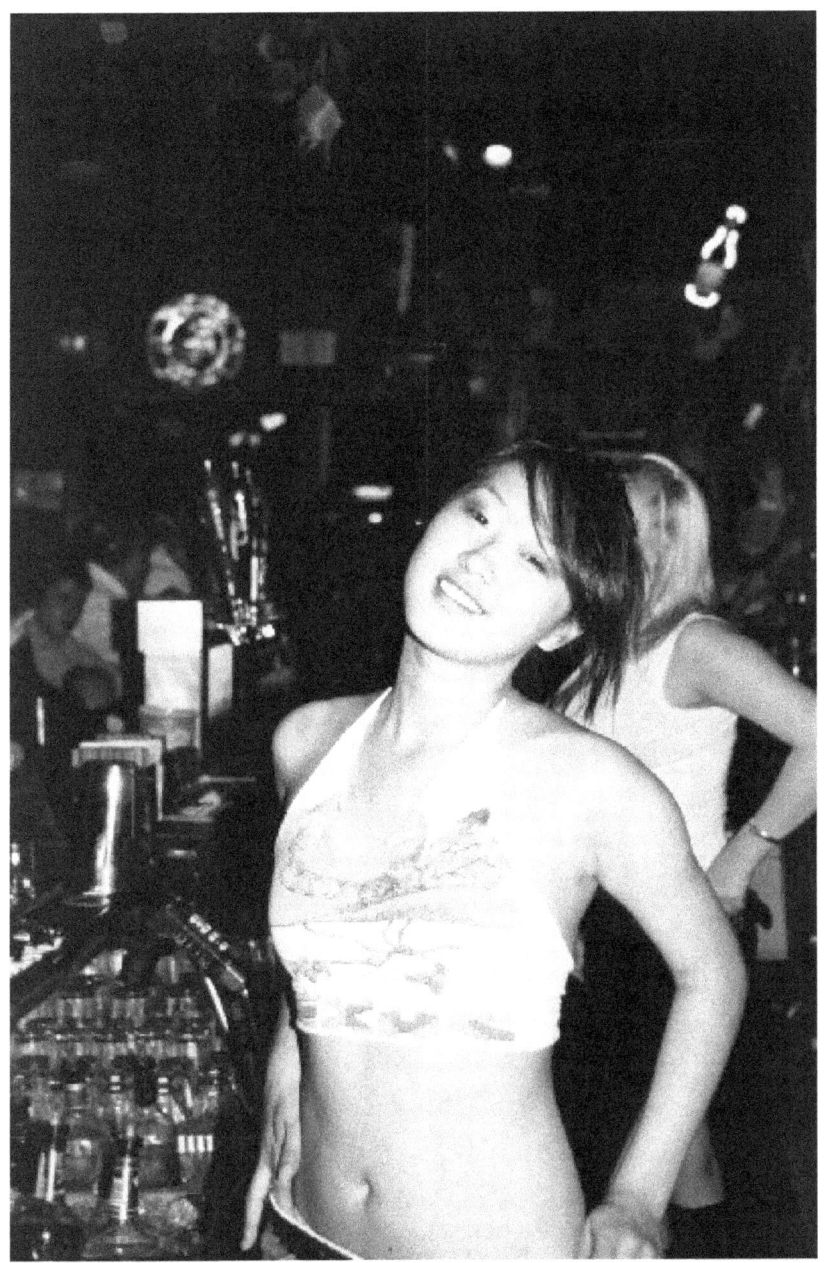

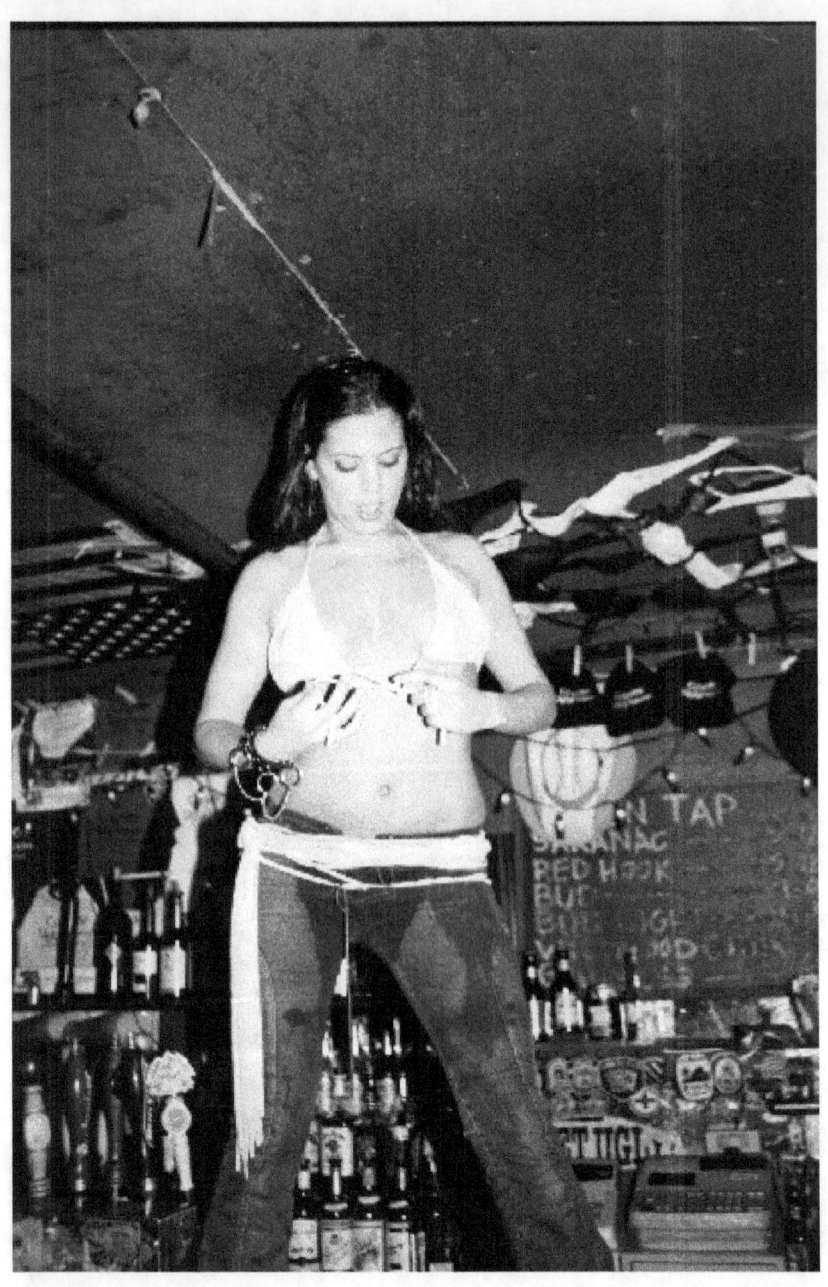

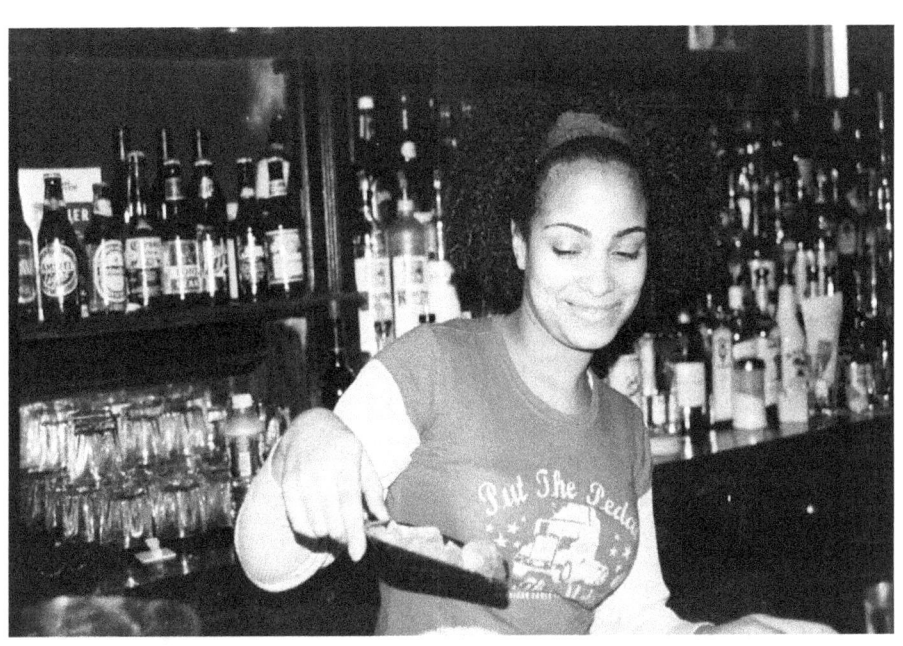

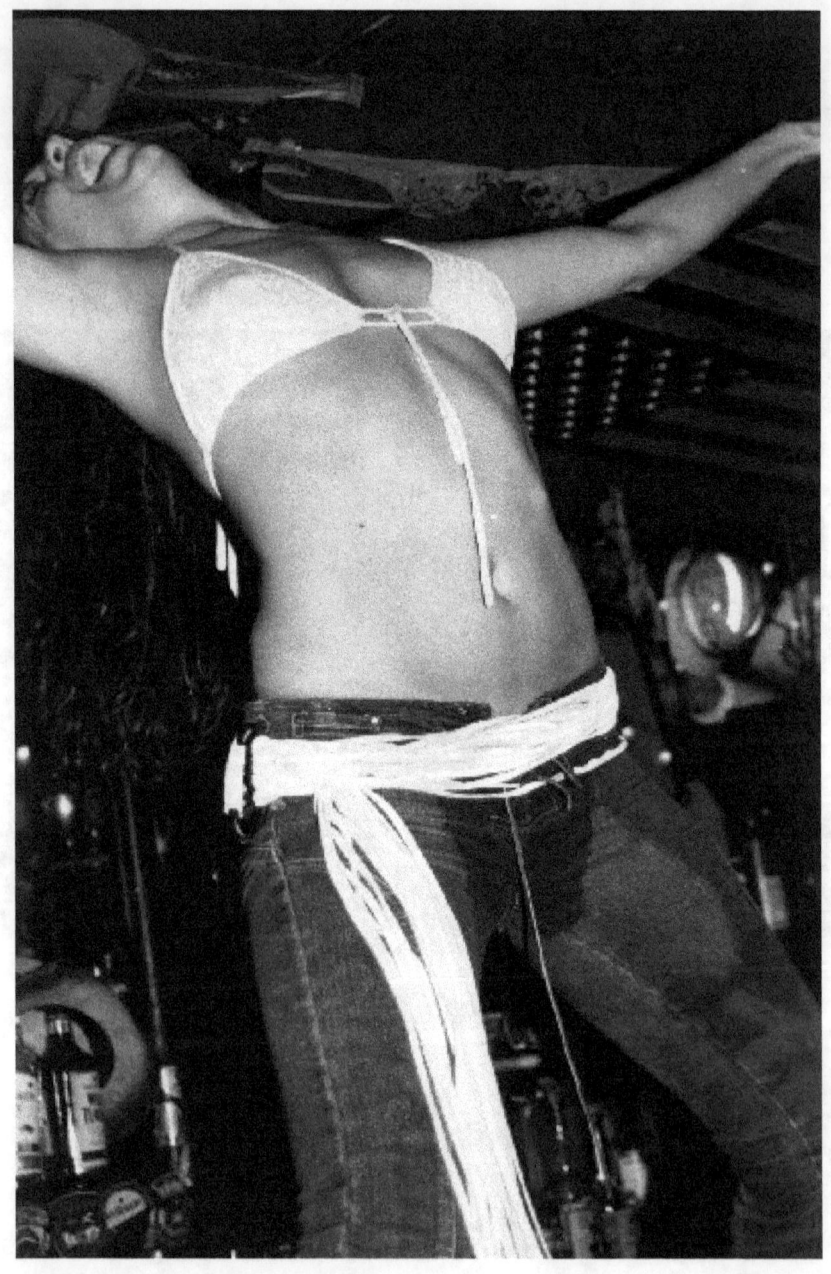

Dedications:

Erik would like to thank all the bartenders for allowing
him to photograph their beauty.

Crazy Legs dedicates this book to Mary Dawn, Patron
Saint of Construction Workers and Short Order Cooks.